"One of the most difficult tas[...] faithful and accessible work t[...] for his readers. Brandon Burks has accomplished that task. Readers of this work will be encouraged to take every thought captive to the obedience of Christ (2 Cor 10:5), that they might be renewed in knowledge, righteousness and holiness (Col 3:10; Eph 4:24). This is a book for everyone in the church, and a book for anyone in the church to give to their friends."

Dr. K. Scott Oliphint, Professor of Apologetics and Systematic Theology, Westminster Theological Seminary

"Pilgrims in a foreign land often provide insights into a place that its natural citizens cannot, or even will not, see. Christians who live as "strangers and exiles on the earth" (Heb 11:13) because of their union with Christ do this today whenever they interpret this fallen world under the light of God's word. *Thinking God's Thoughts* prepares followers of Christ to do just that by surveying an array of biblical truths and showing their significance for believing, thinking, and living well, to the glory of God. May readers see in these pages, and adopt for themselves, that rare combination of biblical content, clarity, compassion, and courage for living in a post-Christian world."

Rev. Dr. Carlton Wynne, Assistant Pastor at Westminster Presbyterian Church (PCA)

"As He speaks in Scripture, the Lord Jesus Christ sets before us a holistic worldview. Expositions of the Christian view of God, man, and salvation; of how Christians ought to think, interpret Scripture, and embrace divine paradox; of how Christians ought to live, order their families, and worship could fill books without number. But to find all of these lifegiving implications of Christianity faithfully presented in one place so intimately intertwined... is what renders Rev. J. Brandon Burks's *Thinking God's Thoughts* a unique treasure. Its design is to help believers explore and indulge what Scripture calls the very 'renewal' of their minds."

Rev. Dr. Brant Bosserman, Minister of Trinitas Presbyterian Church (PCA), Author of *The Trinity and the Vindication of Christian Paradox*

Thinking God's Thoughts

Thinking God's Thoughts

An Introduction to a Pilgrim Worldview

J. Brandon Burks

Fontes Press

Immanuel Kant told the world that "we *must* reason autonomously and must never reason in any other way."[7] The secular world agreed and made Kant's mandate of autonomy one of its chief pillars, claiming that humans must push aside those ancient books and live by their own standards. This book is a direct challenge to this secular view of the world.

The Christian, by contrast, knows that right thinking without God is a fool's errand, affirming with Cornelius Van Til: "We make Scripture the standard of our thinking, and not our thinking the standard of Scripture."[8] Apart from Scripture, our reason is bankrupt. Our minds can only reason properly when they are grounded in the Christian faith, because it is the only story of the world that is not a fantasy.[9]

The Bible and the Trinity form the necessary starting points for knowledge and a basic view of the world.[10] This means that the Christian's fundamental orientation is not inward (the human as ultimate), but outward (God as ultimate). That is, we do not assume for ourselves an authoritative, god-like ability to determine right and wrong, true and false; rather, we begin with Scripture and we let God be God.

Reading the Bible properly and *thinking* biblically go hand in hand. We must read Scripture well so we can think God's thoughts after Him. Surely, our Lord would not want us *believing* like Christians but *thinking* like pagans. This volume seeks to orient the reader's thinking to God's Word and provide tools for handling and interpreting Scripture. In other words, this book is a basic guide to simple principles by which the growing Christian can be helped in his or her understanding of Scripture and also in the application of Scripture to his or her life and worldview.

I have endeavored to keep the discussions very basic in hopes that this book serves the Christian who is beginning to learn, grow, and ask questions. There are times, however, when we will have to delve further into various issues. But this is good, even for those beginning their journey. It is hard to grow without being challenged. The world will challenge us in negative ways. Let us seek to be challenged in positive ways where we can.

One of the fun games to play when teaching children to swim is "submarine." The child gets on the parent's back and they move from one end of the pool to the other. For the majority of the time, the parent's head is above water, but the parent submerges a few times to get the child used to being underwater and holding his or her breath. Hopefully the child does well, but sometimes, without first getting a proper breath, the child might come up coughing and panicking. In a similar way, this book aims to stay above water the majority of the time. But we will submerge on occasion. I hope it doesn't overwhelm you. If you find yourself out of air and panicking, don't give up. Keep reading, thinking, discussing, and praying, asking God to give you understanding. If you don't get everything at first, it's okay. Take what the Lord allows and continue to live by faith in what you *do* know of Him.

This book is divided into three parts. Part I will survey the foundations of a biblical worldview. These are key pillars that will help the Christian properly view God, Scripture, the world, and himself or herself. Part II will give us the ideas and language necessary for keeping proper balance as we seek to understand God's Word. Distinctions and biblical categories will help the catechumen rightly think through the truths of Scripture and then view the world through the lens that Scripture has provided. Part III will survey some practical considerations to give boundaries, motivations, and how-to instructions for the proper handling and application of Scripture.

were written were *not* the mere words of men, but the very Word of God (1 Thess 2:13; 2 Pet 1:20-21). In other words, God wrote a Book. He wrote a Book that is comprised of the sixty-six books of the Old and New Testaments (together referred to as the *canon* of Scripture).[6]

God's characteristics are stamped upon every book in the Bible, which is why both God and His Word are called "faithful and true" (Rev 3:14; 22:6). We use words like *inerrant* and *infallible* to describe the Bible.[7] Inerrancy means that the Bible *does not* err, while infallibility means that it is *impossible* for the Bible to err.[8] To demean or degrade Scripture is to demean or degrade God Himself. To claim that there are errors in God's Word is to claim that there are errors in God, which is impossible (Num 23:19; Ps 145:17). The God of truth cannot lie (Num 23:19; Isa 65:16; Titus 1:2). Therefore, His Word cannot lie or be found untruthful in what it says. God's Word is called "flawless" (Prov. 30:5, NIV), "pure" (Ps 12:6), and "truth" (John 17:17), because these descriptions are true of God Himself.

Still some will quibble, "But what about ancient manuscripts of Bible passages where scribes have made spelling errors?" or, "What about a biblical author who speaks about the sun 'rising,' when we know that the earth revolves around the sun?" How can the Bible be without error with such language? We must caution ourselves not to demand scientific and pedantic precision that the biblical authors never intended.[9] Our weather channels today still say, "The sun will rise at such-and-such a time tomorrow." We know this is not scientifically accurate, but it is accurate *from the point of view of the one speaking.* We call this a *phenomenological* way of talking. The Chicago Statement on Biblical Inerrancy gives this helpful clarification:

WE DENY that it is proper to evaluate Scripture according to standards of truth and error that are alien to its usage or purpose. We further deny that inerrancy is negated by Biblical phenomena such as a lack of modern technical precision, irregularities of grammar or spelling, observational descriptions of nature, the reporting of falsehoods, the use of hyperbole and round numbers, the topical arrangement of material, variant selections of material in parallel accounts, or the use of free citations.[10]

Ultimately, the Bible is *inerrant* and *infallible* because God wrote the Book, and *that* Book is, therefore, our ultimate authority. This means that we cannot verify Scripture by appealing to any standard outside of Scripture—there is nothing higher than the highest authority. We do not hold the sixty-six books of the Bible as the highest authority *because* of a church's opinion, a council's decision, or historical evidence.[11] It is good that we have historical evidence and that the church recognized the canonical books, but these are not the chief reasons why we believe the Bible to be God's Word. The Scriptures, rather, are *self-authenticating* and the very standard of truth.[12]

It follows that Scripture comes with the same *authority* as God Himself. After all, God wrote every word of the Book. The Bible claims nothing less than absolute authority to which we must submit in thought, word, and deed.[13] The authority of the Bible was presupposed by Jesus when He rhetorically asked questions such as, "Have you not read?" (Matt 19:4) or when He proclaimed, "It is written" (Matt 4:4). The Bereans exemplified the authority of Scripture when they made sure that Paul's message complied with God's Word (Acts 17:11).

Some, however, would have you believe that God failed in His task to clearly communicate to His people, claiming that the

Bible is so obscure, so riddled with perplexities, that only a certain class of people can interpret it. To be sure, there are difficult passages in the Bible (2 Pet 3:15-16), but they do not negate its essential *clarity* (or *perspicuity*). The central message of Scripture can be clearly read and understood by the simple.[14] The Word of God "imparts understanding to the simple" (Ps 119:130) and makes "wise the simple" (Ps 19:7).

The Bible is also *necessary*. Humans were created to live in a world where God's revelation in Scripture and God's revelation in nature coincide. Therefore, as Cornelius Van Til famously said, "revelation in nature and revelation in Scripture are mutually meaningless without one another and mutually fruitful when taken together."[15] After Adam sinned against God and humanity fell in Adam, Scripture became all the more necessary, for how else will sinners learn about salvation in Christ (John 20:31; Rom 10:14; 2 Tim. 3:15)?

For some, the Bible is like a holy scrapbook, filled with isolated, unconnected statements of inspiration. This is an inappropriate view of Scripture. All sixty-six books of the Bible are linked together in one *unified* narrative. This is the case because God is the Author of it all. For this reason, Paul can incorporate passages from Genesis, Isaiah, Hosea, and Malachi in a unified way in just one chapter (Rom 9).

The Puritan poet George Herbert wrote beautifully of the Bible's unity:

> Oh that I knew how all thy lights combine,
> And the configurations of their glory!
> Seeing not only how each verse doth shine,
> But all the constellations of the story.[16]

Herbert realized that the Bible is not a holy scrapbook but, ultimately, a unified collection of one Author's work, unified in message as well as authorship. There are parallels between the various texts of Scripture, and when you bring them together, like stars, they paint an entire constellation. Herbert concludes the poem by saying, "This book of stars lights to eternal bliss."[17] The unified message of the Bible is the gospel of Jesus Christ; if one grasps this message by faith, it "lights to eternal bliss."

Scripture is also *powerful* (Acts 6:7; 12:24; 19:20; 1 Thess 2:13). The writer of Hebrews explained that "the word of God is living and active, sharper than any two-edged sword, piercing to the division of soul and of spirit, of joints and of marrow, and discerning the thoughts and intentions of the heart" (Heb 4:12). God declared that when His Word leaves His mouth, "it shall not return to me empty, but it shall accomplish that which I purpose, and shall succeed in the thing for which I sent it" (Isa 55:11). Elsewhere God explained, "I am watching over my word to perform it" (Jer 1:12).

Martin Luther[18] had a keen sense of Scripture's power. As he reflected on the Protestant Reformation (of which he is remembered as one of, if not *the*, primary leader), he declared, "I simply taught, preached, and wrote God's Word; otherwise I did nothing.... the Word did everything."[19] While Luther drank beer in the pub with his friends or slept, the Word was moving, transforming, and carrying out God's purposes. Indeed, it is God's speech that determines reality itself.

Finally, the Bible teaches us that it is *sufficient*. While historical information from other sources can be helpful, the Bible *alone* is sufficient to teach us how to be saved and how to live a godly life. The Bible was able to make Timothy "wise for salvation through faith in Christ Jesus" (2 Tim 3:15). In addition to salvation, the Bible is sufficient for those things "that pertain to life and godliness" (2 Pet 1:3). God's Word is "a lamp to my feet and a light to my path" (Ps 119:105), instructing the godly on how

God is "of Himself" (*a se* in Latin). There is, however, a slight distinction between God's independence and His aseity. The latter term refers only to God's self-sufficiency with regard to His existence, while the former term speaks more broadly of God's independence in everything—from His perfections to His eternal decree to His works in history.[2] This is seen most clearly in Exodus 3:

> Then Moses said to God, "If I come to the people of Israel and say to them, 'The God of your fathers has sent me to you,' and they ask me, 'What is his name?' what shall I say to them?" God said to Moses, "I am who I am." And he said, "Say this to the people of Israel: 'I am has sent me to you.'" God also said to Moses, "Say this to the people of Israel: 'The Lord, the God of your fathers, the God of Abraham, the God of Isaac, and the God of Jacob, has sent me to you.' This is my name forever, and thus I am to be remembered throughout all generations." (Ex 3:13-15)

There is no higher reference point than God Himself. By calling Himself "I AM," God is saying that He is self-contained, self-existing, perfect, complete, and independent. Human beings need many things to keep on living, and we are constantly changing and growing; God does not need anything. Man can say, "I was" and "I will be," but God alone is the great I AM, independent and of Himself.[3]

One of the attributes of God that strains our finite minds is the *infinity* of God. *Infinite*, says A. W. Tozer, "means so much that nobody can grasp it, but reason nevertheless kneels and acknowledges that God is infinite. We mean by infinite that God knows no limits, no bounds and no end. What God is, He is without boundaries."[4] The Psalmist praised the infinite God:

"Great is our Lord, and abundant in power; his understanding is beyond measure" (Ps 147:5). Job, likewise, spoke of God as without limit (Job 11:7-9).

Can you imagine living outside of space and time? Such thoughts are almost entirely incomprehensible for created beings like us. When God created "in the beginning" (Gen 1:1), it included the creation of space and time. Skeptics sometimes ask, "When was God created?" That is a question, however, that only makes sense in time. Without time, the idea of "beginning" does not make sense. God never began to be; He always was. The Psalmist wrote, "Before the mountains were brought forth, or ever you had formed the earth and the world, from everlasting to everlasting you are God" (Ps 90:2). God is an "eternal God" (Deut 33:27) whose years are "unsearchable" (Job 36:26). He declares the end from the beginning (Isa 46:9-11) and has existed "before all things" (Col 1:17). He is immortal (1 Tim 6:16), the first and the last (Rev 1:8).

The independent, infinite, and eternal God is also *immutable* (unchangeable). Change occurs throughout all creation, but God is "the same" (Ps 102:26-27). God does not change (Mal 3:6); He does not change His mind (Num 23:19). In God "there is no variation or shadow due to change" (James 1:17). Mark Jones speaks about the great comfort in knowing that God does not change: "God will be what he is because he is always himself— unchanging in his love toward us because he cannot be anything else to those who are in Christ."[5]

It follows that nothing is too difficult for God (Gen 18:14; Jer 10:12); indeed, nothing is impossible with God (Luke 1:37). God is all-powerful, an attribute we call *omnipotence*. In fact, one of God's names is "Power" (Mark 14:62). Because God can do whatever He pleases (Ps 115:3; 135:6), all things are possible with God (Matt 19:26). Geerhardus Vos defines God's power as the "capacity to put His will into effect outwardly."[6] God is powerful to carry out His will, and nothing can get in His way or stop Him (Dan 4:35).

God is also all-knowing, referred to as *omniscience*. Because God is infinite, His knowledge is without limit (Ps 147:5). God is all-knowing because He both created and planned whatsoever comes to pass (Isa 46:8-11; Eph 1:11). God knows all things past, present, and future (Job 28:24; 37:16; Ps 94:9-10). God knows the intentions of our hearts (Ps 139:23-24) and all of our thoughts (Ps 94:11; 139:1-2). "God knows all things in and of himself," says Herman Bavinck, "He knows all things instantaneously, simultaneously, from eternity; all things are eternally present to his mind's eye."[7] God, who is outside of time, sees the events from Genesis 1:1 to Revelation 21-22, and everything in between, simultaneously.

God is spirit (John 4:24). Though there are other spiritual beings that God created, He is present everywhere, also called *omnipresence*. There is no place a person could go to escape God's presence (Ps 139:7-10; Jer 23:24). This is why Paul could tell the philosophers, "He is actually not far from each one of us" (Acts 17:27). A. W. Tozer rightly said, "God is equally near to all parts of His universe."[8] Jonah thought he could run and hide from God, but he soon found out that God is everywhere (Jonah 1:3, 17). David also had this realization, writing, "Where shall I go from your Spirit? Or where shall I flee from your presence? If I ascend to heaven, you are there! If I make my bed in Sheol, you are there!" (Ps 139:7-8).

Having surveyed several of God's incommunicable characteristics, how should we think about God? Is God just a clump of attributes? Is God the sum total of His parts? Not at all. God has no parts. This belief is referred to as the *simplicity* of God. We are not calling God "simple-minded," but we are affirming that

He is not made up of parts. "All of God does all that God does," says Jones, "God's love is his power is his eternity is his immutability is his omniscience is his goodness, and so forth."[9] Notice the way the Psalmist describes God: "The Lord is gracious and merciful, slow to anger and abounding in steadfast love. The Lord is good to all, and his mercy is over all that he has made" (Ps 145:8-9). As the Psalmist draws attention to one of God's attributes, it leads to mentioning many more, because out of the one fountain flow all of His attributes in harmony.

Thinking biblically begins with a simple and yet profound realization: We are not God. We are like God; we mirror God in many ways. We are made in His image, but we are not God.[10] As these attributes have highlighted, God is greater than we are. This truth was driven home to Job in a profound way when God asked Job a series of questions:

> Who is this that darkens counsel by words without knowledge? Dress for action like a man; I will question you, and you make it known to me. Where were you when I laid the foundation of the earth? Tell me, if you have understanding. Who determined its measurements—surely you know! Or who stretched the line upon it? On what were its bases sunk, or who laid its cornerstone, when the morning stars sang together and all the sons of God shouted for joy? Or who shut in the sea with doors when it burst out from the womb, when I made clouds its garment and thick darkness its swaddling band, and prescribed limits for it and set bars and doors, and said, "Thus far shall you come, and no farther, and here shall your proud waves be stayed"? Have you commanded the morning since your days began, and caused the dawn to know its place, that it might take hold of the skirts of

---

KNOWING OUR PLACE

I f we know God's majestic splendor and dominion, it follows that we will know our place in the created order. John Calvin famously wrote, "Nearly all the wisdom which we possess, that is to say, true and sound wisdom, consists of two parts: the knowledge of God and of ourselves."[1] If God is God and we are not, then we, His creatures, are utterly dependent upon Him. God is the foundation of all life (Ps. 36:9). It is in Him that we live and move and have our being (Acts 17:28).

This dependence impacts everything, including our thinking. We are not just dependent upon God for our daily sustenance, but also for knowing and understanding Him, ourselves, and the world around us. We must, as Van Til was fond of saying, "think God's thoughts after Him."[2] God alone is the Creator. God alone has created and given meaning and a goal to everything that exists, both visible and invisible (Col 1:16). Every fact created by God has God's interpretation stamped upon it. As His creatures, this means that our job is to see everything as God has declared it to be. Our interpretation of things in creation must correspond to God's original interpretation of all things. God has given meaning, purpose, and a goal to all created things and, if we

The serpent was enticing Eve to *judge* or *determine* what is good and what is evil.[7] Will Eve listen to God's declaration of what is good and what is evil, or will Eve usurp God's authority and make those declarations herself?[8] Knowing good and evil is neutral in itself. God's people should know the difference between good and evil. But will Eve know good and evil as a covenant keeper who obeys and follows God, or will Eve know as a covenant breaker who sets up her own standard of truth and has personal experience doing evil acts?[9]

The satanic lie from the beginning is that we can become God and even usurp Him. Unlike Christ, who quoted God's Word when in a similar situation (Luke 4:4, 8, 12),[10] Eve (and later Adam) bought into Satan's program (Gen 3:6). The rest is history, I suppose. All of humanity is born guilty and corrupted by sin. From Genesis to Revelation we see this same Eve-like impulse in fallen man. Was not the tower of Babel an attempt to reach Heaven in a mutinous revolt?[11] Do we not see this same desire in the various pagan kings and kingdoms?

Since Genesis 3, a competing standard and foundation for thinking and reasoning entered the mind of man (Gen 3:22). Instead of thinking God's thoughts after Him, the sinner will interpret all of life apart from and contrary to God and His Word.[12] In other words, ever since Adam rebelled against God, fallen humans have judged God and His creation based upon their own minds, their own thoughts, and their own reasoning.

Autonomous thought is thinking and reasoning apart from the authority of God and His Word.[13] Humans were not designed to think or reason outside of God's authority; we were never meant to be a law unto ourselves. God created everything and gave meaning and purpose to everything He created. If we want to understand this created world rightly, we must understand it through the lens of Scripture.[14]

At this point, some may be saying, "So are you claiming that I can't use my brain?" Not at all. God made the brain to do wonderful things. However, reason must know its proper place if it is going to reason according to its God-given design. The Word of God, says Scott Oliphint, must set the "boundaries and provide the proper structure within which our thinking is to operate."[5] From the beginning, God's revelation was designed to form the foundation for man's thinking.[6] The launching pad for our reason was designed to be none other than God's authoritative Word. In fact, apart from the biblical narrative, nothing in the created order can be understood properly.[7] The only appropriate posture of a creature of God is a child-like trust (Matt 18:1-6):

> Trust in the Lord with all your heart, and do not lean on your own understanding. In all your ways acknowledge him, and he will make straight your paths. Be not wise in your own eyes; fear the Lord, and turn away from evil. (Prov 3:5-7)

If we boil it down, there are two ways of thinking. We can think in humble submission within the boundaries of God's revelation, or we can think in a more Eve-like way, making ourselves the final standard for right and wrong, true and false. For the Christian, there is no question on this point. Jesus said, "My sheep hear my voice, and I know them, and they follow me" (John 10:27). Our redeemed instinct is to follow that voice and not to hold on to our would-be autonomy. Jesus has the words of life; where else can we go?

Sadly, many refuse to follow Jesus as they attempt to forge their own way based upon their own standards. They give their own minds an authority that should only belong to God. Imagine what it would look like to learn things if there were no God.

The human mind would attempt to be ultimate and bring all the disconnected, chance-produced facts of the universe together. How would all the facts relate to one another? How could one know something to be true if one's mind did not know all facts? Incorporating new facts into our "pool of knowledge" would inherently change or reorient the things we know. Without God, the human mind would have to know all facts of the cosmos in order to know just one fact with any degree of certainty. But the human mind is incapable of being a unifier on this grand of a scale, which would undermine the autonomous person's confidence in knowing anything at all. As Van Til rightly said, "Every fact *must stand in relation to other facts* or it means nothing to anyone."[18] Therefore, there must be something outside of the human mind that brings all the facts of the created order together in a coherent way.[19] Fortunately, knowledge is possible for humans because Christ has created all things and "holds together" all things (Col 1:17).

The universe was created by God and is held together and governed by Him; for this reason, the laws of physics and the laws of logic—the created order itself —reflects His character. We can know and reason and understand because we are made in the image of God. God has brought every created fact, every law of nature, every truth in the universe together. Because God is the Creator, He not only knows all truths but also knows how every truth relates to every other truth.[20] Those who would follow the serpent and choose rebellious autonomy can never be sure they truly know anything, but those who humbly submit to the authority of the all-knowing God can begin to attain to "the knowledge of God and of ourselves."

In this chapter, we have seen that God is God and we are not. That is, we are not autonomous creatures. We cannot climb the heights of knowledge in our own strength, as Eve attempted. We are utterly dependent creatures in both life and salvation. God's revelation must form the foundation and starting place for all of our thinking and reasoning. If we are to understand God, ourselves, and the world in which we live, we must humble ourselves and submit to God and His Word. As God tells us, "But this is the one to whom I will look: he who is humble and contrite in spirit and trembles at my word" (Isa 66:2). In the next chapter, we will consider the differences between God's revelation in Scripture and God's revelation in nature.

> I am evil, born in sin;
> thou desirest truth within.
> Thou alone my Savior art,
> teach thy wisdom to my heart.
> Make me pure, thy grace bestow,
> wash me whiter than the snow.[21]

SCRIPTURE AND THE COSMOS

A farmer wakes up one morning. The sun is out. No rain clouds are in sight. He sips his morning coffee, looks up to Heaven, and thanks God: "Thank you Lord! You have given me a bountiful harvest this season!" His neighbor, who happens to be an atheist, overhears this farmer and retorts, "God did not give you this harvest! It was the good soil, the sun, and all that rain we've been having."

Who is correct, the Christian farmer or the atheist neighbor? Did God give the farmer the bountiful harvest, or was it the product of the good soil, sun, and rain? Of course, this is a trick question, because it is not either/or. The atheist neighbor did not contradict the Christian farmer. Rather, the atheist neighbor highlighted the way in which God worked to bless the farmer. God used the soil, the sun, and the rain as means to bestow a bountiful harvest (cf. Ps 67:6).

When summer gives way to autumn, and autumn to winter, and winter to spring, we see the very speech of God at work. Indeed, we are reminded that Christ "upholds the universe by the word of his power" (Heb 1:3). We are accustomed to thinking about God speaking creation into existence (Ps 33:9), but we

are not so accustomed to thinking about God governing, direct-
ing, and sustaining all of creation by His speech as well.

God's Word not only creates; it also sustains and governs
creation. The latter action is referred to as *providence.*[1] God's
providence comes through a type of "speech" that is inaudible,
but the effects are clearly seen all around us.

Scripture teaches, "He sends out his command to the
earth; his word runs swiftly. He gives snow like wool; he scat-
ters frost like ashes" (Ps 147:15-16). God "sends out his word" and
the winds blow and waters flow (Ps 147:18). "He made a decree for
the rain," says Job (28:26). God "utters his voice" and there is rain,
wind, and thunder (Jer 10:13). In fact, all things that providentially
happen come from God's "mouth," and they are "spoken" (Lam
3:37-38). These things include the seasons, the rain, and the harvest (Jer 5:24). God also upholds and guides the animals (Ps 29:9;
104:27; Matt 6:26). Nothing is outside of God's governance.

Since God both created and governs all things by His Word,
we can understand science as that which studies the speech of
God governing the universe.[2] The regularity that we see in nature is God's governing speech at work. It is no wonder that the
scientific laws, such as the laws of physics, bear the reflection of
God's own attributes.[3] The various laws of nature appear to us as
being all-powerful, all-present, and so on. This makes sense, giv-
en the fact that God is the Creator and sustainer of the laws of
nature—they necessarily reflect His glory and power.

As we look to the night sky, or as we backpack across a
mountain range, or as we just enjoy a simple picnic in the park,
we see the beauty and glory of God on display. Consider Psalm
19:1-6 (emphasis added):

> The heavens *declare* the glory of God, and the sky
> above *proclaims* his handiwork. Day to day *pours out*

speech, and night to night *reveals knowledge*. There is no speech, nor are there words, whose voice is not heard. Their *voice* goes out through all the earth, and their *words* to the end of the world. In them he has set a tent for the sun, which comes out like a bridegroom leaving his chamber, and, like a strong man, runs its course with joy. Its rising is from the end of the heavens, and its circuit to the end of them, and there is nothing hidden from its heat.

Here we see the speech of God working in creation, revealing and proclaiming His glory. Similarly, Romans 1:20 teaches that "his invisible attributes, namely, his eternal power and divine nature, have been clearly perceived, ever since the creation of the world, in the things that have been made." It is evident from these texts that both Scripture and nature are considered God's *revelation*.[4] The Belgic Confession expresses the Bible's teaching on this very nicely:

> We know God by two means: First, by the creation, preservation, and government of the universe, since that universe is before our eyes like a beautiful book in which all creatures, great and small, are as letters to make us ponder the invisible things of God: God's eternal power and divinity, as the apostle Paul says in Romans 1:20. All these things are enough to convict humans and to leave them without excuse. Second, God makes himself known to us more clearly by his holy and divine Word, as much as we need in this life, for God's glory and for our salvation.[5]

Theologians often make a distinction between *general* revelation and *special* revelation. Special revelation refers to God's

Word in written form, namely, the Bible.[6] General revelation, says Vern Poythress, is "what God shows to all human beings through his actions of creation and providence."[7] Because God is the Author of both, general and special revelation must form a cohesive unit. But what happens when a scientific theory contradicts the Bible? We must keep in mind that while general revelation is infallible, scientific theories are the "fallible *interpretations*" of God's speech in and through creation.[8]

If you pick up a science textbook written in the early to mid-1900s, it will be evident that scientific theories are fallible: they change, they morph, they "evolve." Special and general revelation, on the other hand, are infallible. Both are the *speech* of God, one in written form and the other in creation and providence.

Nevertheless, the question still remains: What do we do when a scientific theory is at odds with the Bible? If science studies the speech of God governing the world, and that revelation is infallible, what do we do when science appears to be at odds with God's written Word? First, we go back to our study of nature to make sure we are interpreting the evidence properly. Then we go back to Scripture to ensure that we have interpreted the text properly. There can be an initial push-and-pull as we consider and re-consider our study of general and special revelation.[9]

However, at the end of the day, the Bible takes priority. The written Word is much clearer than viewing the *effects* of God's speech in creation and providence. Not only this, but Romans 1:20 indicates that general revelation renders humanity "without excuse." Fallen humans clearly behold the attributes of God in creation, but they suppress that truth in unrighteousness (Rom 1:18-23). General revelation, therefore, has a *negative* effect on the sinner. There is no defect in God's revelation, but there is a defect in the sinner's response to it and interpretation of it. In short, we can conclude: A scientific theory is a fallible human interpretation of the divine Word in general revelation, whereas the Bible *is* the divine Word itself.[10] Of course, the Bible still has to be interpreted and can be interpreted incorrectly, but it is far more clear and specific than general revelation by itself.

Think about Adam in the Garden of Eden. What if God never verbally warned him about which tree bore inappropriate fruit? Adam would not have known his covenantal duty, nor would he have had hope in the blessed life to come. Adam needed special revelation in order to know the dangers of the tree of the knowledge of good and evil. But what if God warned Adam of the tree of the knowledge of good and evil without general revelation? Adam would not have known what a tree was. For Adam to recognize special revelation, he needed general revelation.[11]

The Bible and the created order are not at odds. If there is a problem, that problem is with us. Van Til rightly taught that God's revelation in nature and God's revelation in Scripture "form God's one grand scheme of covenant revelation of himself to man," and neither Scripture nor nature was ever meant to be isolated from the other.[12]

▼

In this chapter we have seen that God reveals Himself both in Scripture and through creation. We call this *special revelation* and *general revelation*, respectively. Both are the products of God's speech. Scripture is God's Word in written form, while creation and providence are God's inaudible speech that governs and sustains all of creation. Both modes of revelation form a unit because, ultimately, they come from the same Author's mouth. Far from being a hindrance to science, understanding God's role in the natural world actually ignites scientific study. As Poythress said, "God has more to show us, and more with which to bless us, in the realms of science and mathematics."[13] After all, "It is the glory of God to conceal things, but the glory of kings is to search things out" (Prov 25:2).

O Lord my God,
when I in awesome wonder
consider all the world thy hands have made,
I see the stars,
I hear the rolling thunder,
thy pow'r throughout
the universe displayed.
Then sings my soul,
my Savior God, to thee:
How great thou art,
How great though art![14]

THE NATURAL AND THE SPIRITUAL

B elievers and unbelievers think differently. "But wait a second," someone might say, "I work with unbelievers and we do the same job and have the same understanding of what we're doing. How is our thinking *different*?" It is true that both the believer and the unbeliever are made in God's image and live in God's world. Nevertheless, as we have seen in previous chapters, the unbeliever suppresses the truth of God (which he knows deep within) and makes himself the ultimate judge of what is true and false, right and wrong.[1]

After Genesis 3, sin affected every area of a person's being. Human emotions, human thinking, human relationships, and so on were marred by sin. The Fall left all individuals guilty of Adam's sin (Rom 5:12-19),[2] corrupted by sin's power (Gen 8:21; Ps 51:5; John 8:34), separated from God (Isa 59:2), and spiritually dead (Eph 2:1; Col 2:13). The only hope for a fallen individual is to be united to the risen Christ by the Spirit and through faith so that the benefits of salvation (justification, adoption, sanctification, and so on) can be applied to the penitent believer.[3]

With the Fall of the human race, anomalies and problems encroached upon God's "very good" creation (Gen 1:31). Death him, and he is not able to understand them because they are spiritually discerned." The natural person belongs to "this age," and the spiritual person (i.e., the person who has the Holy Spirit) belongs to the "age to come."[19] There is a great divide (or "antithesis") between the natural and spiritual person (Prov 9:10; 24:7). The "things of the Spirit" are discernable and assessable only through the Spirit's activity, which means that apart from revelation and the work of the Spirit, the natural person cannot have *right* knowledge of anything.[20] Without God and His Word, "*it is impossible to prove anything,*" writes Bahnsen. He continues: "The atheist world view is irrational and cannot consistently provide the preconditions of intelligible experience, science, logic, or morality."[21]

There is a massive gulf or antithesis between the natural person (unbeliever) and the spiritual person (believer). Scott Oliphint taught that there will be aspects of the "truth of the knowledge of God that surface in those who are in Adam [i.e., the 'natural man']."[22] Oliphint continues,

> So, for example, even though an unbeliever will recognize that two plus two equals four, the very fact that he would hold that truth to be independent of God's creating and sustaining activity means that he does not know that truth as it really is. This may not affect the equation itself, but neither will God say to him on judgment day, "Good for you; you got that part right." Those who die in Adam will be held responsible for every fact (even "two plus two equal four") that they took from God's world, even as they refused to acknowledge the facts to be God's facts in the first place.[23]

Because of the great divide between believer and unbeliever, there is no common ground or neutral territory in which they might come together. The Christian presupposes God and His Word as ultimate while the unbeliever presupposes himself as ultimate. But if this is the case, is it hopeless for a believer to try to persuade an unbeliever of the truthfulness of Christianity? Absolutely not! How will they believe unless someone preaches the gospel to them (Rom 10:14)? But in our evangelism and persuasion, we do not want to encourage the unbeliever to think in autonomous ways or to stand in judgment over God and His Word.[24] Rather, we want to encourage the unbeliever to submit to the Triune God, who created all things and sustains all things. In fact, we ought to demonstrate that unless the unbeliever presupposes the God of sacred Scripture, nothing could be known at all.[25]

The point of contact between the believer and unbeliever lies in the fact that the unbeliever is made in the image of God. Van Til wrote, "The point of contact for the gospel, then, must be sought within the natural man. Deep down in his mind every man knows that he is the creature of God and responsible to God. Every man, at bottom, knows that he is a covenant breaker."[26]

———————▼———————

In this chapter we have seen that, after the events of Genesis 3, all of humanity can only be described as *fallen*. Humanity, after the Fall, is dead and corrupted by sin. The natural man suppresses the knowledge of God (though imperfectly) and makes himself the ultimate standard of truth. He does not understand the things of the Spirit, because the things of the Spirit require him to have the Holy Spirit. But when the Spirit of Christ redeems a fallen sinner through faith, he or she becomes designated a *spiritual person*—that is, a person in whom the Holy Spirit dwells. The redeemed sinner is now in direct contrast

———————▼———————

In this chapter we have seen that God condescended to us by way of covenant. The history of God's dealings with humanity is a *covenantal* history, and that covenantal history has an end-goal in view, namely, the New Heavens and New Earth. Adam, in the Garden, was oriented toward this New Heavens and New Earth, a place even better than Eden. The overarching plan of God is summed up well by Lane Tipton: "God seeks to confer Himself in a communion bond upon a holy people in a holy realm and advance them beyond probation through an obedient representative."[27] Adam failed to be the obedient representative that would bring humanity into God's rest (Heb 4:1-11). To enter God's rest, Jesus, the second Adam, needs to redeem fallen sinners through His own obedience and blood. Humanity is now divided into two camps: those in Adam (covenant breakers) and those in Christ (covenant keepers). Those in Adam will be eternally condemned and those in Christ will live forever with Him. In the next chapter, we consider how the Triune nature of this covenant God shapes our worship and worldview.

O Lord, haste the day
when my faith shall be sight,
the clouds be rolled back as a scroll;
the trump shall resound,
and the Lord shall descend.
Even so–
It is well with my soul.[28]

A TRINITARIAN WORLDVIEW

A s Christians, we believe there is only one God. One of the doctrines that separates us from Judaism and Islam, however, is that we believe that there is Trinity in unity, or three Persons in the Godhead. The doctrine of the Trinity is not only the foundation for existence (*principium essendi*)[1] but also impacts our life and worldview. The Trinity is foundational to the Christian faith, but it is a truth that we cannot fully comprehend.

The early church spent much time thinking and deliberating about issues and complexities surrounding the Trinity. Sometimes the language they used can seem too academic, too "ivory-tower." However, the questions they were asking and the creeds they were writing were motivated by the desire to worship the correct God. Scott Oliphint rightly says,

> The questions about the identity of Christ were questions, in the first place, not simply about correct doctrine, but about thinking properly in order to *worship* properly. The church was not concerned about doctrine for doctrine's sake, nor should we be. Instead,

they were intent on worshiping the one, true God as He had revealed Himself; to worship any other god would be to worship a false god, not the true God of history and redemption.... We simply cannot understand *how* it can be that God is one and three, but we affirm it with all of the vigor and certainty that Scripture requires of us.[2]

Scripture is clear that there is only one God. "You believe that God is one; you do well. Even the demons believe—and shudder!" (James 2:19; cf. Deut 6:4; 32:39; 1 Cor 8:6). But the one, true God is Trinity. This is evident throughout the New Testament:

> To those who are elect exiles of the Dispersion in Pontus, Galatia, Cappadocia, Asia, and Bithynia, according to the foreknowledge of God the Father, in the sanctification of the Spirit, for obedience to Jesus Christ and for sprinkling with his blood. (1 Peter 1:1-2)

> The grace of the Lord Jesus Christ and the love of God and the fellowship of the Holy Spirit be with you all. (2 Corinthians 13:14)

> In the beginning was the Word, and the Word was with God, and the Word was God. He was in the beginning with God. (John 1:1-2)

> And when Jesus was baptized, immediately he went up from the water, and behold, the heavens were opened to him, and he saw the Spirit of God descending like a dove and coming to rest on him; and behold, a voice from

heaven said, "This is my beloved Son, with whom I am well pleased. (Matthew 3 :16-17)

These texts (and others) instruct us as to who God is: He is Father, Son, and Holy Spirit. Matthew 28:19 is another important text: "Go therefore and make disciples of all nations, baptizing them in the name of the Father and of the Son and of the Holy Spirit." You will notice that Jesus did not say "names" (plural) but "name" (singular). The *one* name of God is Father, Son, and Holy Spirit.

But what about the Old Testament? Are Jesus and the Holy Spirit in the Old Testament? Yes, both Jesus (Gen 16:7-13; 18:1-2; Judg 5:23) and the Holy Spirit (Gen 1:2; Ps 51:11; Zech 7:12) are seen in the Old Testament.[3] B. B. Warfield said this of the Trinity in the Old Testament:

> The Old Testament may be likened to a chamber richly furnished but dimly lighted; the introduction of light brings into it nothing which was not in it before; but it brings out into clearer view much of what is in it but was only dimly or even not at all perceived before. The mystery of the Trinity is not revealed in the Old Testament; but the mystery of the Trinity underlies the Old Testament revelation, and here and there almost comes into view. Thus the Old Testament revelation of God is not corrected by the fuller revelation which follows it, but only perfected, extended and enlarged.[4]

Throughout the Bible, we are told that there is one God in three Persons—Father, Son, and Holy Spirit—and that each Person is fully and completely God. The Father is God (Rom 15:6; 2 Cor 1:3-4; 1 Pet 1:3), the Son is God (Acts 20:28; Rom 9:5; Titus 2:13), and the Holy Spirit is God (Acts 5:3-4; 1 Cor 2:10-12; Heb 3:7-11). But, again, there is only one God (Deut 6:4).

In the Trinity there is only one *essence* (one *substance*) and three *Persons* (three *hypostases* or *subsistences*).[5] Each Person is God in and of Himself: co-eternal, co-equal, and co-authoritative.[6] The Father is unbegotten, the Son is begotten of the Father, and the Holy Spirit proceeds from the Father and the Son.[7] Each person also mutually indwells each other without confusion (called *perichoresis;* John 10:30; 14:10).[8]

Again, we do not fully comprehend these truths. Perhaps we can rest with Gregory of Nazianzus, who said, "I cannot think on the one without quickly being encircled by the splendor of the three; nor can I discern the three without being straightway carried back to the one."[9] Holding both the one and the three in our minds will help us avoid overemphasizing unity over diversity or diversity over unity.

In fact, many of the ancient heresies had a tendency to overemphasize one aspect of the Trinity. *Arianism* taught that the Father and Son were *similar* (*homoiousios*) in substance but not of the *same* (*homoousios*) substance. *Modalism* taught that there is one God in three forms or roles but not three Persons. *Tritheism* taught that there are three Gods: Father, Son, and Holy Spirit. *Partialism* taught that God is one-third Father, one-third Son, and one-third Holy Spirit.[10]

To help protect the biblical teaching of the Trinity, the early church penned The Athanasian Creed, named after Athanasius (AD 293–373). Therein, they rightly decreed:

> (1) Whosoever will be saved, before all things it is necessary that he hold the catholic[11] faith; (2) Which faith except every one do keep whole and undefiled, without doubt he shall perish everlastingly. (3) And the catholic

faith is this: That we worship one God in Trinity, and
Trinity in Unity; (4) Neither confounding the persons, nor
dividing the substance. (5) For there is one Person of the
Father, another of the Son and another of the Holy Spirit.
(6) But the Godhead of the Father, of the Son, and of the
Holy Spirit is all one, the glory equal, the majesty co-
eternal. (7) Such as the Father is, such is the Son and such
is the Holy Spirit. (8) The Father uncreate, the Son uncreate, and the Holy Spirit uncreate. (9) The Father incomprehensible, the Son incomprehensible, and the Holy
Spirit incomprehensible. (10) The Father eternal, the Son
eternal, and the Holy Spirit eternal. (11) And yet they are
not three eternals, but one eternal. (12) As also there are
not three uncreated nor three incomprehensibles, but
one uncreated and one incomprehensible. (13) So likewise the Father is almighty, the Son almighty, and the Holy Spirit almighty; (14) And yet they are not three almight-
ies, but one almighty. (15) So the Father is God, the Son is
God, and the Holy Spirit is God; (16) And yet they are not
three Gods, but one God. (17) So likewise the Father is
Lord, the Son Lord, and the Holy Spirit Lord; (18) And yet
they are not three Lords, but one Lord. (19) For like as we
are compelled by the Christian verity to acknowledge
every person by himself to be God and Lord; (20) so are
we forbidden by the catholic religion to say: There are
three Gods or three Lords. (21) The Father is made of
none, neither created nor begotten. (22) The Son is of the
Father alone; not made nor created, but begotten. (23)
The Holy Spirit is of the Father and of the Son; neither
made, nor created, nor begotten, but proceeding. (24) So
there is one Father, not three Fathers; one Son, not three
Sons; one Holy Spirit, not three Holy Spirits. (25) And in

this Trinity none is afore, nor after another; none is greater, or less than another. (26) But the whole three persons
are co-eternal, and co-equal. (27) So that in all things, as
aforesaid, the Unity in Trinity and the Trinity in Unity is
to be worshipped. (28) He therefore that will be saved
must thus think of the Trinity.[12]

There are, however, different ways we can speak about the
Trinity, and we should be clear in how we are speaking. For example, sometimes we zoom in and look at who and what the
Trinity is in and of itself (called the *ontological Trinity*), and other times we examine the mission of the Trinity in creating and
in redeeming falling sinners (called the *economic Trinity*). In
other words, we can speak of God in Himself (*ontological*) and
also of God in relation to His creation (*economic*).

Why are these two aspects important to distinguish? Because there are truths about the Trinity that relate to creation
and redemption that do not relate to the Trinity in and of itself.[13]
An example of this is the Son submitting to the Father's will.
Jesus said in John 6:38, "For I have come down from heaven, not
to do my own will but the will of him who sent me." Similarly, 1
Corinthians 11:3 says that, "the head of Christ is God." This is true
of the Trinity regarding redemption (when Jesus took on flesh
to obey unto death; cf. Phil 2:8), but it is not true of the Trinity in
and of itself.[14] The Godhead has only one will, one power, and
one operation—the Godhead works inseparably in all that God
does.[15]

When God the Son took on flesh (John 1:14), humbling Himself by taking the form of a servant (Phil 2:7), there was no
change in God (for God is immutable). When we look at the
Trinity in relation to creation and the redemptive mission, we
see Jesus, the Son of God, suffering and dying, being crushed by

the Father (Isa 53:10; Matt 27:46); we see Him being led by the Spirit and living by faith.[16] These things are aspects of the *economic* Trinity but not the *ontological* Trinity. It would be an error, for example, to see Jesus submitting to the Father in accomplishing redemption and then conclude that Jesus is eternally *subordinate* to the Father.[17]

With these distinctions in mind, let us turn to a basic question: How does the Trinity impact our worldview? Most basically, the Trinity is our foundation and starting point. Van Til said, "This conception of God is the foundation of everything else that we hold dear," and he went on to rightly declare, "Any other sort of God is no God at all."[18]

The Father, Son, and Holy Spirit love each other and communicate with each other, and this forms the foundation for our love, communication, and reception of divine revelation.[19] Even our language reflects the Trinity. Vern Poythress wrote, "Language reflects the character of God and Trinitarian structure *all the way down*. Both the complexities of human communication, complexities of long discourses, and the seeming simplicity of a single word reflects Trinitarian mystery."[20] You might even say that we speak because God has spoken.[21]

Have you ever wondered why our world is filled with unity and diversity? We look at a husky and a poodle and yet we say "dog." So many things are diverse, and yet so many things are united. In the Trinity, unity and diversity are *equally ultimate*; one does not take priority over the other.[22] John Frame says, "There is no oneness without manyness.... creation does in important ways reflect God's unity and diversity. No human philosopher will ever discover in the world a unity without plurality.... Nor will they discover a plurality without a oneness that defines its nature."[23] Because the universe was created by a Triune God, it reflects the Three-in-One character of God.

———————▼———————

This chapter has helped us to think biblically about who God is and what that means for our worldview. There is only one God, but that one God is in three Persons, and each Person is fully and completely God. Our human minds are not able to grasp the range of what this means; however, it is foundational to our faith and worship. The God who created, covenanted, and redeemed is a Triune God. The Trinity accounts for so much of our world, from our ability to love, to our ability to speak, to our ability to understand God's revelation to us.

Holy, holy, holy!
Lord God Almighty!
All thy works shall praise thy name
in earth and sky and sea.
Holy, holy, holy!
Merciful and mighty!
God in three Persons,
Blessed Trinity![24]

PART II

CATEGORIES AND DISTINCTIONS

_____

KEEPING BALANCE AND SEEKING COHESION

P roblems arise when we take one truth from God's word and then bulldoze over the rest of Scripture. An example of this might be grasping the truth that Jesus is man and then deducing that He cannot be of the *same* substance with the Father (Arianism), or by grasping the Oneness of God and rejecting the Threeness.

When we think through Scripture, we must maintain balance. Cornelius Van Til rightly said that the Christian should "take all the factors of revelation into consideration simultaneously."[1] Obviously, no one is going to know the Bible so perfectly and so exhaustively that he will be able to hold every single truth in his mind simultaneously. What Van Til is teaching is that we must keep balance and think according to the texts of Scripture, so as not to become unbalanced or abstract in our thinking. A few examples will give us a clearer picture:

Example One: Must Pastors Be Married?

In 1 Timothy 3, Paul says that an overseer (pastor) must be the "husband of one wife," and he must keep "his children submissive" (vv. 2, 4). Does this mean that a pastor *must* be married and have children? No, not at all. The apostle Paul said in 1 Corinthians 7 that there are circumstances in which it is better not to marry, so as to allow one to focus more intently on the things of God (vv. 26-28, 32-35). Therefore, *if* a pastor is married, he must not be promiscuous; and *if* a pastor has children, he should manage his household well. We bring these two texts together and keep balance.

Example Two: How Did Judas Die?

In Matthew's Gospel, it is written that Judas "went and hanged himself" (27:5). But in the Book of Acts, it says that Judas fell headlong and "burst open in the middle and all his bowels gushed out" (1:18). Do we have here a contradiction in the Bible? Not at all. These are not *contradictory* accounts but *complementary* accounts. Derek Thomas writes, "To Matthew's account, Luke adds that Judas was apparently allowed to hang until a degree of decomposition had taken place. Thus, when the body fell to the ground, it burst open."[2] These truths are meant to be brought together.

Example Three: Does God Work or Do We?

Some people tend to think that either God works or we work—His efforts *or* our efforts. We run to one extreme where we anxiously toil, trusting in our own strength. Or, we rest upon God so much that we don't do anything; we become lazy and unfruitful. Here, again, we must maintain balance.

In Philippians Paul tells the church to continue to "work out your own salvation with fear and trembling, for it is God who works in you, both to will and to work for his good pleasure"

(2:12-13). We are called to work diligently, but Paul wants to make sure that we are not trusting in our own strength. We work "with fear and trembling," the appropriate attitude when in the presence of someone with authority (cf. Mark 5:33; 2 Cor 7:15; Eph 6:5). He commands us to work *because* God is working inside of us, to choose and to toil according to His pleasure. Who is at work, you or God? This text says *both*. We could even say: in *our* working, *God* is working. Our good works, as believers in Christ, are Spirit-wrought works, but they are still our works (Gal 5:22-23; Eph 2:10).[3] Because God is at work, we need not be anxious; rather, we should have the utmost confidence that our labors, done in faith to the glory of God, will not be fruitless.

Example Four: Does Learning Help or Hurt?

We are aware of the famous saying in the opening chapter of Ecclesiastes, "For in much wisdom is much vexation, and he who increases knowledge increases sorrow" (Eccl 1:18). The apostle Paul also warns that knowledge puffs up (1 Cor 8:1). Perhaps, if we only read these passages, we might conclude that ignorance is best. Maybe we should not be wearied by so many books (Eccl 12:12)?

However, if this conclusion were true, what would we make of Solomon commanding us elsewhere to get wisdom, promising that wisdom leads to a happy life and is better than gold?[4] How would we understand churches being rebuked for a lack of growth in knowledge and understanding (1 Cor 3:2; Heb 5:11-6:2)? If Christ is our wisdom (1 Cor 1:30), we need not despise or avoid wisdom. Still, there is a difference between *godly* wisdom and *worldly* wisdom (Col 2:8; James 3:13-18).

In Ecclesiastes, Solomon is brought to sorrow with the increase of knowledge and wisdom because he came to see more of the fallenness of God's once "very good" creation. No amount of human wisdom can solve the world's problems; the only solution is the wisdom that comes from God embodied in His Son, Jesus Christ (Eccl 2:26; 1 Cor 1:30).[5] Divine wisdom is so antithetical to the wisdom of the world that the world cannot help but think of God's wisdom as "foolishness" (1 Cor 1-2). The children of God should, with all humility and with a desire to serve others, sit at the feet of Christ and learn as much as they can from the pages of Scripture. Indeed, books can be a good thing that will aid in acquiring wisdom and understanding (2 Tim 4:13; cf. Prov 17:16; 23:23).

Example Five: Do We Need Good Works or Not?

The Bible teaches us that we are justified (i.e., declared righteous) by faith alone (Rom 4; 5:1; Gal 2:15-16; 5:4). Our sins have been pardoned and we have been declared to be righteous because Jesus has imputed His righteousness to us, which we have received by faith alone. Even so, we are still sinners (Rom 7:15-25; 1 John 1:8-9). Until Jesus returns or calls us home, we will sin. It would be wrong, however, to conclude that we can persist in living sinful, rebellious, and unrepentant lives and be saved (Matt 7:17; 1 Cor 6:9-10; 1 Pet 4:1-11).

Jesus said, "If you love me, you will keep my commandments" (John 14:15; cf., 15:10). Paul teaches that "if by the Spirit you put to death the deeds of the body, you will live" (Rom 8:13). James warned that "faith by itself, if it does not have works, is dead" (James 2:17). And John states more explicitly, "Whoever makes a practice of sinning is of the devil.... No one born of God makes a practice of sinning, for God's seed abides in him; and he cannot keep on sinning, because he has been born of God" (1 John 3:8-9).[6]

It is true that a sinner is saved by faith apart from works (Eph 2:8-9; Titus 3:5), but faith is never without repentance and good works (Eph 2:10). Jesus said to "repent and believe in the gospel" (Mark 1:15). Repentance is the turning from sin and the hating of sin.[7] The doctrine of justification by faith alone can never be used to excuse sin or to become lazy in our good works (Matt 7:17-20; Eph 2:10). Many carnal people are comforting themselves that they will go to Heaven *without* repenting of sin and pressing on in Spirit-wrought good works (Matt 7:21-23; John 3:36; Gal 5:22-23; James 2:17-26).[8] What did Paul tell the church at Corinth?

> Or do you not know that the unrighteous will not inherit the kingdom of God? Do not be deceived: neither the sexually immoral, nor idolaters, nor adulterers, nor men who practice homosexuality, nor thieves, nor the greedy, nor drunkards, nor revilers, nor swindlers will inherit the kingdom of God. And such were some of you. But you were washed, you were sanctified, you were justified in the name of the Lord Jesus Christ and by the Spirit of our God. (1 Cor 6:9-11)[9]

At one time, the Christians at Corinth were enslaved to these sins. Sin characterized these Christians before they repented and trusted in Christ for their salvation. They were "washed," "sanctified," and "justified." This does not mean they never struggled with these sins after conversion; it does not mean they were never tempted by these sins after being united to Christ. The church is indeed a hospital for sinners, but it is not a haven for the impenitent (Matt 18:15-20; 1 Cor 5:5, 9-13; 2 Thess 3:6, 14-15).

There is a difference between struggling with sin and living in sin. There is a difference between putting our sin to death and celebrating it. Christians are not sinless, but neither do they continue to live the lifestyle they once lived when they were outside of Christ (Rom 6:1-2; 1 Pet 1:13-16; 4:1-11).[10] Sin is to be mortified and put to death, for it is a deadly poison that ravages the heart, mind, and life. John Owen famously said that the Christian should "always be killing sin or it will be killing you."[11] If a person is comfortably living in unrepentant sin, these words of Paul should be a warning: "The unrighteous will not inherit the kingdom of God." Likewise, the writer of Hebrews meant what he said: "...without holiness no one will see the Lord" (Heb 12:14, NIV).

Example Six: Does God Hate the Sinner or the Sin?

What do we make of the famous saying: "God loves the sinner but hates the sin"? Is it true that God merely hates the sin one does, rather than the sinner himself? How do we understand God's love relative to the sinful acts of sinners?

It is true that God is love (1 John 4:8) and that He loved a sinful and rebellious world so much that He sent His Son to die in order to redeem sinners (John 3:16; Rom 5:6, 8). It is also true that God gives common grace[12] to the just and the unjust alike—He sends the rain, sunshine, and other such blessings to both believer and unbeliever (Matt 5:45). Not only this, but Jesus invites all sinners, "Come to me, all who labor and are heavy laden, and I will give you rest" (Matt 11:28).

But can we say that God *only* hates sin and *not* the sinner himself? We cannot say this.[13] The Bible affirms God's hatred toward not only the sin committed but the *sinners* who commit those sins.[14] Consider a few verses that highlight this reality:

> For you are not a God who delights in wickedness; evil may not dwell with you. (Psalm 5:4)

The Lord tests the righteous, but his soul hates the wicked and the one who loves violence. (Psalm 11:5)

There are six things that the Lord hates, seven that are an abomination to him: haughty eyes, a lying tongue, and hands that shed innocent blood, a heart that devises wicked plans, feet that make haste to run to evil, a false witness who breathes out lies, and one who sows discord among brothers. (Proverbs 6:16-19)

In Hell, God is not punishing abstract sins but *people* who have sinned and have not come to Christ in faith and repentance. Revelation 21:8 attests, "But as for the cowardly, the faithless, the detestable, as for murderers, the sexually immoral, sorcerers, idolaters, and all liars, their portion will be in the lake that burns with fire and sulfur, which is the second death." It will be unrighteous sinners who experience God's wrath for all of eternity. They will not inherit the Kingdom of God (1 Cor 6:9-10) but will remain outside the gates of Heaven: "Outside are the dogs and sorcerers and the sexually immoral and murderers and idolaters, and everyone who loves and practices falsehood" (Rev 22:15).

God can love us with the intent to save us, even while "hating God-despising rebels like us."[5] Before God saved us by grace, we were under God's just and righteous wrath (John 3:36; Rom 16:7; Eph 2:1-10). God can love us because, at one time, He despised His own Son (Isa 53:10-12; Mark 15:33-41). "He made the one who did not know sin to be sin for us, so that in him we might become the righteousness of God" (2 Cor 5:21, CSB). Those who are outside of Christ, however, will experience the eternal hatred of God, which is completely pure and just.

This can all sound macabre and dreary. How can we find any joy in the hatred of God? We can find joy, however, when we

or sister to stumble (Rom 14:21; 1 Cor 6:7). In other words, while an abstainer might sin against a partaker by passing judgment, the partaker should be compelled by love to abstain while around that particular brother or sister for the sake of his or her conscience.

—————— ▼ ——————

Troubles ensue when we get off balance. Many of the problems or pitfalls the church has faced happened when individuals took one truth in Scripture to the exclusion of all the others. The Bible has but one ultimate Author. The Holy Spirit does not make *contradictory* statements but *complementary* statements. All the truths of the Bible cohere, so let us bring them together in harmony. The next chapter encourages us to let the texts of Scripture form the boundaries of our thinking so that we avoid abstract speculations that damage the texts of Scripture.

> Holy Spirit, dwell with me:
> I myself would holy be;
> separate from sin, I would
> choose and cherish all things good,
> and whatever I can be,
> give to him who gave me thee![21]

THINK CONCRETELY

When I was a young child, an aunt referred to me as the "what-if boy." All day long I riddled her with "What if?" questions, wanting to know all the hypothetical scenarios that, given the proper conditions, just might happen. As you can imagine, many of my questions were too abstract and unrealistic to merit a response.

Sometimes Christians riddle God or their pastors with such questions. But the Christian is not called to think in the abstract or to dabble in the overly speculative (Ps 131:1-2). The Christian is to reason *concretely*, according to the text of Scripture (Deut 29:29). If we "reason concretely about God and his relation to the world," says Cornelius Van Til, "we simply listen to what God has told us in his Word on the matter."[1]

We think abstractly or speculatively when we fail to balance the truths of Scripture. We see one truth in the Bible and say, "Therefore, this must needs be the case," while doing damage to other truths in Scripture. We must avoid the temptation to conclude with a speculative "therefore" when the Bible does not draw the same conclusion. The Christian will do well to mind the words of John Calvin:

Let us, I say, allow the Christian to unlock his mind and
ears to all the words of God which are addressed to him,
provided he do it with this moderation, viz., that whenever the Lord shuts his sacred mouth, he also desists from
inquiry.[2]

To give an example, the Bible portrays God as absolutely
sovereign and in full control, even over the actions of His creatures. Consider the following passages:

Your eyes saw me when I was formless; all my days were
written in your book and planned before a single one of
them began. (Psalm 139:16, CSB)

I am God, and there is none like me, declaring the end
from the beginning and from ancient times things not yet
done, saying, "My counsel shall stand, and I will accomplish all my purpose..." (Isaiah 46:9-10)

In him we have obtained an inheritance, having been
predestined according to the purpose of him who works
all things according to the counsel of his will. (Ephesians
1:11)

Some have read these passages and have asked, "Why should
I pray if God has planned everything and controls everything?
After all, Matthew 6:8 says that God knows what I need before I
even ask." But this is to reason in the *abstract* and to draw con-
clusions the Bible never draws. What do the Scriptures say? The
Bible says that we should be devoted to prayer (Acts 2:42; Col
4:2), that God hears our prayers (1 John 5:14-15), that God answers prayer (Ps 107:13; Mark 11:24), that the prayer of a righteous

person is powerful (James 5:16), and that we lack things because we have failed to pray for them (John 16:24; James 4:2-3). Nowhere in the Bible are we encouraged not to pray because God is sovereign, all-knowing, and in full control. In fact, it is *because* God is sovereign, all-knowing, and in full control that we are encouraged to pray and bring our requests before God.[3] Herman Witsius rightly said, "Whatever benefits he [God] has decreed to bestow upon us, he has decreed to bestow in answer to prayer."[4]

Another example where people tend to think abstractly is regarding God's sovereignty in salvation and evangelism. Scripture declares that Salvation is "of the Lord," not of man (Jonah 2:9). We are told that God "chose us in him before the foundation of the world, that we should be holy and blameless before him. In love he predestined us for adoption as sons through Jesus Christ, according to the purpose of his will" (Eph 1:4-6), and that salvation "depends not on human will or exertion, but on God, who has mercy" (Rom 9:16). In fact, after Peter preached the gospel, only those who "were appointed to eternal life believed" (Acts 13:48).

These texts amplify the fact that God is in control of everything, including salvation (*monergism*). If this is the case, why do we evangelize? If God elects some people to be saved, then why do we take the gospel to the nations? If God is saving people, can we stay home and never share the gospel?

By no means! Scripture says, "How then will they call on him in whom they have not believed? And how are they to believe in him of whom they have never heard? And how are they to hear without someone preaching? And how are they to preach unless they are sent?" (Rom 10:14-15). And elsewhere, "If I say to the wicked, O wicked one, you shall surely die, and you do not speak to warn the wicked to turn from his way, that wicked person shall die in his iniquity, but his blood I will require at your

without the illumination and inspiration of the Holy Spirit... one is deceived by the heretical spirit.... To love God is completely a gift of God. (Canons 1, 5, 7, 25)[9]

But does God not predestine and elect *based upon* His foreknowledge? Some have taught that God looked down the "tunnel of time" and saw who, out of their own free will, would choose Him. God *then* elected or predestined, they say, those whom He saw would come to Him in faith. One passage that may seem to support this view is Romans 8:29: "For those whom he foreknew he also predestined to be conformed to the image of his Son."

However, this passage does not teach that God merely knows in advance who will choose Him.[10] This is clear for at least three reasons. First, God does not elect people based upon foreseen faith in them, because no one can believe in God unless that person is born again by His Holy Spirit. John Piper put it like this: "Man is dead in trespasses and sins. So there is no condition he can meet before God chooses to save him from his deadness."[11] If God merely looked down the "tunnel of time," all He would see is spiritually dead people unable to choose Him (Rom 3:9-19; 8:7-8; 1 Cor 12:3).[12] Secondly, the text does *not* say, "those whom He foreknew would believe in Him from their own free will." There is no indication that this qualification needs to be added to this text. *All* those foreknown are predestined, *all* those predestined are called, *all* those called are justified, and *all* those justified are glorified (Rom 8:29-30).[13] Thirdly, the "foreknown" in Romans 8:29 is another way of saying "foreloved." This is the way the Bible often speaks about *knowing* someone (cf. Gen 18:19; Jer 1:5; Amos 3:2). Douglas Moo, a prominent New Testament scholar, suggests that this verb ("foreknow") in Romans 8:29 means to "enter into a relationship with before," to "choose, or determine, before," or to "know intimately."[14]

All those unlovable sinners who were loved by God in eternity past—based upon God's will alone (Eph 1:5)—were predestined to salvation. They will be, in time, effectually called, justified, and, eventually, glorified when Jesus returns.[15] If God chose you as the apple of His eye in eternity past, He will overcome every obstacle to be with you, including your own deadness and unbelief.[16] This is a humbling and heart-warming truth.[17] The Westminster Confession of Faith expresses it well:

> These angels and men, thus predestinated, and foreordained, are particularly and unchangeably designed, and their number so certain and definite, that it cannot be either increased or diminished. Those of mankind that are predestinated unto life, God, before the foundation of the world was laid, according to his eternal and immutable purpose, and the secret counsel and good pleasure of his will, hath chosen, in Christ, unto everlasting glory, out of his mere free grace and love, without any foresight of faith, or good works, or perseverance in either of them, or any other thing in the creature, as conditions, or causes moving him thereunto; and all to the praise of his glorious grace.... The doctrine of this high mystery of predestination is to be handled with special prudence and care, that men, attending the will of God revealed in his Word, and yielding obedience thereunto, may, from the certainty of their effectual vocation, be assured of their eternal election. So shall this doctrine afford matter of praise, reverence, and admiration of God; and of humility, diligence, and abundant consolation to all that sincerely obey the gospel. (3.4, 5, 8)[18]

Scripture teaches that salvation is a work of the Trinity. The Father graciously chooses some Hell-bound sinners for salvation

(Eph 1:4-6), the Son dies for those elect who were given to Him by the Father (John 6:39; 10:15), and the Holy Spirit applies the salvation purchased by Christ to the elect (Rom 8:30).[19] Instead of leading us to ask, "Why should I evangelize?", this truth should motivate us to say with Paul, "I endure everything for the sake of the elect, that they also may obtain the salvation that is in Christ Jesus with eternal glory" (2 Tim 2:10).

If one thinks abstractly and speculatively, either the sovereignty of God or the responsibility of man will be suppressed or denied. The Bible, however, demands that we hold both together *at the same time*. The progress of history and our choices are real and meaningful. At the same time, God planned and decreed it all. God has elected some sinners for salvation, and yet the gospel is really offered to everyone to whom it is proclaimed. We must allow these tensions to remain, lest we do damage to the Bible's teaching.[20]

So far, we have considered concrete thinking when it comes to understanding biblical truths: We say what Scripture says, and we stop our minds from vain and abstract speculation. But what about applying Scripture to our lives? What lesson does concrete thinking give to us regarding our Christian worldview? In what way can we get pulled into speculation?

One example from history is the Salem Witch Trials. The Puritans were spiritual giants and some of the most devout, godly, and pious writers you may ever read. They rightly saw, for example, the evils and danger of witchcraft (Lev 19:31; Deut 18:9-14; Acts 19:19; Gal 5:19-21). However, some were given over to vain speculation. One such Puritan was Cotton Mather. He held to outlandish beliefs about the nature and powers of a witch, and spoke of suckling imps, witches' marks, and signing the devil's book. But what led him to such beliefs? It was the unexplainable experiences that occurred before his eyes, coupled with the testimonies of others. Mather felt at ease incorporating this "knowledge" into his theological belief system. Mather wrote,

> That we are safe, when we make just as much use of all Advice from the invisible World, as God send it for. It is a safe Principle, That when God Almighty permits any Spirit from the unseen Regions, to visit us with suprizing [sic] Informations, there is then something to be enquired after; we are then to enquire of one another, What Cause there is for such things? The peculiar Government of God, over the unbodied Intelligences, is a sufficient Foundation for this Principle.[21]

Joel Beeke and Randall Pederson write that Mather's book *On Witchcraft* was highly speculative: "While Mather had a heart for sound piety, he often indulged in speculation. This is Mather at his worst."[22] Trying to live by wild speculations from the "invisible world" and mixing biblical truth with "truths" from the unseen spiritual realm is a fool's errand. A better (and safer) course of action would have been to think concretely and to live by God's revealed will as outlined in Scripture. After all, The Westminster Shorter Catechism affirmed, "The duty which God requireth of man, is obedience to his revealed will."[23]

———▼———

Christ has not called us to think abstractly; He has called us to hear His voice and follow Him (John 10:27). We are to think concretely, to constantly ask, "What do the texts say? What do the Scriptures teach?" In this chapter we have seen that God is absolutely sovereign and in total control of everything, because He planned everything in eternity past (Isa 46:10). But here the

When my dim reason would demand
why that, or this, thou dost ordain,
by some vast deep I seem to stand,
whose secrets I must ask in vain...
Be this my joy, that evermore
thou rulest all things at thy will;
thy sov'reign wisdom I adore,
and calmly, sweetly, trust thee still.[21]

CAUSES AND RESPONSIBILITY

P arents occasionally hear, "That's not fair!" Their child is claiming that, from his or her perspective, a matter was not handled justly. Similarly, there are times when we are tempted to ask, is God dealing fairly with us or with others?

In chapter nine of Romans, Paul knows that the reader will have trouble with what he is teaching. We may even say to God, "This is not fair!" Paul writes:

> For this is what the promise said: "About this time next year I will return, and Sarah shall have a son." And not only so, but also when Rebekah had conceived children by one man, our forefather Isaac, though they were not yet born and had done nothing either good or bad—in order that God's purpose of election might continue, not because of works but because of him who calls— she was told, "The older will serve the younger." As it is written, "Jacob I loved, but Esau I hated." What shall we say then? Is there injustice on God's part? By no means! For he says to Moses, "I will have mercy on whom I have mercy, and I will have compassion on whom I have compassion." So then it

depends not on human will or exertion, but on God, who has mercy. For the Scripture says to Pharaoh, "For this very purpose I have raised you up, that I might show my power in you, and that my name might be proclaimed in all the earth." So then he has mercy on whomever he wills, and he hardens whomever he wills. (Rom 9:10-18)

Paul knows what the reader must be thinking: If God hardens people's hearts and chooses people for salvation before they were born, how is anyone responsible? Paul knows this question is coming, and he rebukes the reader because it is an inappropriate question: "You will say to me then, 'Why does he still find fault? For who can resist his will?' But who are you, O man, to answer back to God? Will what is molded say to its molder, 'Why have you made me like this?' Has the potter no right over the clay, to make out of the same lump one vessel for honorable use and another for dishonorable use?" (9:19-21).

When everyone deserves wrath—when everyone deserves Hell—the salvation of even *one* person would be very gracious of God. The fact that He has elected multitudes magnifies His mercy and grace. The elect are shown mercy and the reprobate are shown justice, but neither are dealt with unjustly.[1]

But here too we must think *concretely*. God is not the author of sin (1 John 1:5), God is sinless (Deut 32:4), God tempts no one (James 1:13), and God is good (Ps 34:8).[2] These truths must never leave our minds. God ordained all things and we are still responsible; we cannot claim that God tempted us or is somehow the author of sin (which is blasphemy!).[3] D. A. Carson explains:

God... stands behind good and evil asymmetrically. To put it bluntly, God stands behind evil in such a way that not even evil takes place outside the bounds of his sovereignty, yet the evil is not morally chargeable to him; it is always chargeable to secondary agents, to secondary causes. On the other hand, God stands behind good in such a way that it not only takes place within the bounds of his sovereignty, but it is always chargeable to him, and only derivatively to secondary agents.[4]

A few more examples from Scripture will help us to understand this principle.

Example One: Who Hardened Pharaoh's Heart?

Let us apply this truth to the hardening of Pharaoh's heart in Exodus. John MacArthur points out, "Ten times (4:21; 7:3; 9:12; 10:1, 20, 27; 11:10; 14:4, 8, 17) the historical record notes specifically that God hardened the king's heart, and ten times (7:13, 14, 22; 8:15, 19, 32; 9:7, 34, 35; 13:15) the record indicated the king hardened his own heart."[5] Who hardened Pharaoh's heart? According to the text, both God and Pharaoh himself. But if God hardened his heart, how can Pharaoh be held responsible? Because the Pharaoh, choosing to harden his own heart, acted sinfully.[6]

It helps us to understand this text if we distinguish between the *ultimate* (or *remote*) cause and the *proximate* (or *immediate*) cause.[7] God is the *ultimate* cause of everything that happens. This means that God sovereignly hardened Pharaoh's heart (Ps 105:24-25). Still, Pharaoh hardened his own heart; he was the *proximate* cause. The Latin term *concursus* means "to run together." Both the ultimate and the proximate cause *run together*. When the Pharaoh chose to harden his heart, there was *concursus* taking place. God ordained that Pharaoh's heart would be hardened so that he would not release Israel, but Pharaoh's choice to harden his own heart was genuine. God's cause was

Satan used seemingly natural agents to carry out the affliction: armed men, fire, and a great wind (1:13-19). Did Job look to the wind and the armed men as the cause of his affliction? Did Job look merely to Satan for what had transpired? No, Job knew that afflictive providence had come upon him from God.[9]

Job said, "The Lord gave, and the Lord has taken away" (1:21), and also, "Shall we receive good from God, and shall we not receive evil?" (2:10). When disputing with his friends, Job was steadfast: "Though he slay me, I will hope in him" (13:5). And in the closing of the book we read, "All his brothers, sisters, and former acquaintances came to him and dined with him in his house. They sympathized with him and comforted him concerning all the adversity the Lord had brought on him." (42:11, CSB). There is no doubt as to who was the ultimate cause of Job's suffering. Despite the evil that Satan meant in harming Job, God meant it for good (Job 42:12-17; Rom 8:28-30).

Example Six: Who Planned Jesus' Death?

Finally, let us consider the murder of the Son of God. That Jesus would be crucified for sinners was a part of God's eternal decree. This eternal decree in no way destroyed the real offer of eternal, consummative life held out to Adam if he obeyed. God did not *force* Adam and Eve to sin and for humanity to fall. Even so, it was decreed by God that Adam would sin, that humanity would fall, and that the Son of God would save sinners. There is no "Plan B" with God. The world we now live in is and always has been "Plan A."[10] Still, we must keep in our minds the meaningful progress of history and real contingency, even while we affirm the all-controlling plan of the sovereign God who is working all things for His glory and our good.[11]

Scripture declares that wicked, culpable, "lawless" men murdered Jesus according to the "definite plan and foreknowledge of God" (Acts 2:23). We are told that God "predestined" all the persons involved in the crucifixion of Christ, from Herod to Pontius Pilate, along with the Gentiles and the people of Israel (Acts 4:27-28). Even the book entitled "The Book of Life of the Lamb Who Was Slain" was written before creation (Rev 13:8).[12] All those whose names were not written in *that* book will commit idolatry and worship worldly powers in defiance of Christ.[13]

———————▼———————

A great mystery is presented to us in Scripture. This mystery is not meant simply for academics to debate but for the Christian to cherish in his or her heart. The Holy Spirit wants the church to know that God is the *ultimate* cause of everything, that God has predestined whatsoever comes to pass, including the dust that floats in the air and the molecules in distant galaxies. From micro to macro, God has predestined it all, including the thought life of his creatures. In a word, there is nothing outside of God's eternal decree. Yet we must have caution and realize with Calvin that when predestination is discussed, "numberless unholy and absurd thoughts rush into the mind."[14] We should say what Scripture says and no more. God is the ultimate cause, but He is wholly good and not the author of sin or the tempter of man; God is the ultimate cause, but we, His secondary agents, are responsible for the things we choose. The Holy Spirit wants us to know this, so let us happily hold this tension and go no further. The next chapter will teach us how to understand God's will regarding good and bad events.

that this Holy Scripture contains the will of God completely"
(Article 7).[3]

Humans are not meant to live according to the sovereign will
of God because we have no way of knowing what it is. We are to
live according to His revealed will. In our sinfulness, we often
wish to peer into that secret counsel of God, but, as Martin Luther reminds us, "This will is not to be inquired into, but rever-
ently adored, as by far the most awesome secret of the Divine
Majesty." Of those secret and hidden things, Luther says,
"[T]here we have no concern."[4]

Take Romans 12:2 for example: "Do not be conformed to this
world, but be transformed by the renewal of your mind, that by
testing *you may discern what is the will of God*, what is good and
acceptable and perfect" (emphasis added). Is Paul calling us to
learn how to predict the future? Not at all. Paul wants us to
know what *ought* to happen tomorrow, not what *will* happen
tomorrow.[5]

Romans 12:2 is speaking about the *revealed* will of God.
However, there are other texts that describe God's *sovereign* will
(e.g., 1 Chron 19:13; Matt 26:39; 1 Pet 3:17). One example is Ephesians 1:11, where Paul says that God "works all things according
to the counsel of his *will*" (emphasis added). So, the Bible speaks
of God's *will* in both ways.[6]

Herman Bavinck brings clarity to the "two will distinction" as
it comes to bear on the existence of evil. The quotation is
lengthy but worthy of meditation:

> Although evil is under God's control, it cannot in the
> same sense and in the same way be the object of his will
> as is the good. There is a big difference between the will
> of God that prescribes what we must do (Matt. 7:21; 12:50;
> John 4:34; 7:17; Rom. 12:2) and the will of God that tells us

what he does and will do (Ps. 115:3; Dan. 4:17, 25, 32, 35; Rom. 9:18-19; Eph. 1:5, 9, 11; Rev. 4:11).... Failure to grant this distinction or some variation of it runs the risk of making God the author of sin and fails to accord to human beings rational, moral responsibility before God.... But God's revealed (preceptive) will is not really his (ultimate) will but only the command he issues as the rule for our conduct. In his preceptive will he does not say what *he* will do; it is not the rule of *his* conduct; it does not prescribe what *God* must do, but tells us what *we* must do. It is the rule for *our* conduct (Deut. 29:29). It is only in a metaphorical sense, therefore, that it is called the will of God. The revealed will is the way the hidden will is brought to realization. It is in the same way of admonitions and warnings, prohibitions and threats, conditions and demands that God carries out his counsel, while God's secret will only ensures that human beings violating God's commandment do not for a moment become independent of God, but in the very moment of violating it serve the counsel of God and become, however unwilling, instruments of his glory. Those who deny God's revealed will fail to take sin seriously; denying the hidden will undermines faith in God's sovereignty.[7]

The two wills of God help us to understand why, for example, God forbids adultery (Ex 20:14), but yet He wills, sovereignly, that adultery be committed by sinful people (John 8:1-11; Rom 9:19-23; Eph 1:11). The two wills of God also help explain how God can desire all to be saved (1 Tim 2:4), and yet all are not saved (Rev 21:8).[8] This has perplexed people throughout the history of the church. How can we understand God's desire for all to be saved, and yet believe that God has not sovereignly willed

the salvation of all people? How do we understand the relationship between God's eternal decree and God's revealed will or
desire? Scott Oliphint helps us navigate this perplexity:

> God delights in the fulfillment of His preceptive will. He
> does not delight in the death of the wicked because wick-
> edness is in opposition to His character. Yet, His eternal
> decree includes His ordaining the reality of death and of
> wickedness; everything is ordained by Him. In all of this,
> God is not working against Himself. Instead, He is, in the
> context of His all-encompassing, universal decree, ex-
> pressing and revealing His own character, in light of what
> He has given to us in His Word.... Though God's decree
> and desire need to be seen in a mysterious tandem, we
> have to recognize the priority of decree over desire. Be-
> cause God's decree initiates *everything* that comes to pass
> in and through His creation, it is His sovereign decree
> that provides the foundation for the 'well-meant' offer of
> the gospel.[9]

Let us return to thinking about suffering, abuse, trials, and
death. God is sovereign over all things (Job 12:10; Ps 135:6; Prov
16:33; Eph 1:11) including calamities, evil acts, and death (Deut
32:39; Isa 45:7; Lam 3:37-38; Amos 3:6). This means that these
acts are a part of His sovereign will, His eternal decree.[10] If these
calamities and acts of suffering *ultimately* come from God's
hand, how does this keep us from despair when evil acts happen
to us?

What might we say to someone who was sexually abused?
First, it must be said that God hates what happened. He is
against it. The perpetrator *is* guilty and wicked, and God will
bring His perfect justice to bear upon that person if he or she

does not repent. God did not approve of the abuse; He did not *force* the person to violate another person. The perpetrator is sinful and lawless.

However, we must also believe that God is so sovereign in that moment that He can turn everything for our eternal good.[11] Our temptation is to push God out of the picture when an evil act occurs, but this only deepens the hurt that we feel. If we push God away, how can He help us? If God did not govern *that* moment, how can He govern any other moment in our lives? When bad things happen to us, we need a God who says, "I am against that sin and if you don't repent, vengeance is mine." And we need a God who is totally sovereign and in control, a God who is folding all the events of our lives—good and bad—into His purposes for us, which is our ultimate joy and goodness in Christ Jesus, our Lord.[12]

Another way to say this is that God can look at an event through two lenses.[13] God can look at a calamity or suffering though a narrow lens and grieve at the sight of it. He does not delight in the death of the wicked (Ezek 33:11), He does not approve of women boiling their children (Lam 4:10), and He is horrified that a man would rape his sister (2 Sam 13:14). For us too, as we zoom in on these atrocities, we grieve, weep, and are horrified.[14]

But God can also look through a wide-angle lens and see the atrocity in connection with everything else. He can see the suffering and how it will unfold for His glory and our joy. God looks at the fallenness of this world and sees redemption in Christ, He sees the coming consummation of all things, and He says, "Very, very good." For us, the wide-angle lens keeps us from getting tunnel vision whereby we miss the big picture and end up in despair.

We are not called to be masochists, enjoying pain and suffering. We are called, rather, to pan out, look at the whole picture,

Thou hast the true and perfect gentleness,
no harshness hast thou and no bitterness:
make us to taste the sweet grace found in thee
and ever stay in thy sweet unity.[18]

Redemptive History and Intrusion

I was asked by an atheist, "If you care about the Bible so much, then why are you not stoning Sabbath-breakers? And how is that even moral to begin with?" He knew that I believed the Bible to be God-breathed and without error, but he was perplexed as to why I do not follow *everything* in the Bible. If the Bible says to stone Sabbath-breakers (Num 15:35), then why would I not obey this command? Besides, how do we understand the morality of stoning people for such an offense?

An understanding of redemptive history (or *biblical theology*) helps to resolve the issue of stoning Sabbath-breakers. God's revelation in Scripture has *unfolded* over the course of history. The reader of Scripture must, therefore, seek to understand how the story of redemption organically unfolds throughout the history of God's special revelation.[1] Timothy Brindle, following Geerhardus Vos, wrote that

> God's redemptive revelation in the earlier parts of Scrip-
> ture were like an acorn that organically grew into a huge
> oak tree by the close of the canon. In other words, as God
> revealed more and more about His plan of salvation, that

acorn grew into a shrub, then in the next era of redemptive history it was a small tree, so that finally, with the
coming of Christ, it is now a full-blooming oak tree. This
means that the acorn had the same 'DNA' as the full-
blooming oak tree all along, and in this sense they are organically unified: thus the Scriptures were always about
Christ![2]

The Scriptures are united in their focus on Christ, but devel-
opments were introduced over the course of redemptive history: The New Heavens and New Earth, a place better than Eden,
was held out to Adam and, in him, to all of humanity. When
Adam failed his probationary test and broke the Covenant of
Works, salvation became necessary in order to reach consummation. Only through the second Adam, Jesus Christ, will sinners be able to enter the consummation that was initially extended to Adam in the Garden. But before Christ takes on flesh,
God's people undergo a time of great anticipation for the coming Messiah.

In the Old Testament, the coming Christ is seen in shadows,
types, and promises. For example, the Passover Lamb that Israel
regularly sacrificed was a foretaste of Christ, our Passover Lamb
(1 Cor 5:7), who took away our sins once and for all (Heb 9:26).
When Israel celebrated the Passover, they were looking upon a
shell.[3] But the core (or the "nut") inside the shell was from the
future. Passover symbolized, embodied, and pointed to a future reality that would one day unfold in God's redemptive
plan.[4]

The future *intruded* or broke through into their present
world. The Fall brought a period of pain and sorrow, but even
still consummation was breaking through (or *intruding*) into the
present.[5] With these intrusions, the "earthly shells" embodied and

signified (like a sacrament), heavenly realities to the Old Testament saints.[6]

In Scripture, we see intrusions of both Christ's first coming (e.g., Passover) and His second coming (e.g., the conquest of Canaan, stoning Sabbath-breakers, etc.).[7] When it comes to the latter intrusions, we must remember how horrific the second coming of Christ will be. So gruesome will Christ's vengeance and justice be (Rom 12:19-20), that His robe will be splattered with the blood of His enemies (Rev 19:13).[8] The second coming of Christ will be a dreadful and awesome sight to behold, as He comes to gather His church and punish those who are not His people (2 Thess 1:8-9).

For this reason, when we see intrusions of the last judgment in the Old Testament, we are likewise horrified. Meredith Kline says that in the conquest of Canaan, "the ethical principles of the last judgment intruded" into history; and when the death penalty was required for religious offenses, it was because "consummation justice" intruded into that redemptive point in time.[9] These intrusions (along with all the disasters and trials of a fallen world; cf. Luke 13:1-9; Rev 8:1-13)[10] lead us to anticipate the judgment to come and to repent while there is still an opportunity.

Another intrusion from the age to come is the Holy Spirit. The age to come (the New Heavens and New Earth) is a Spirit-saturated realm. Every time a sinner is born again, there is Spirit intrusion. This means that the Holy Spirit was present in both the Old and New Covenants, saving sinners by grace through faith. The Holy Spirit, however, has a greater presence in the New. David Murray teaches that in the Old Testament, the Spirit's presence was like a water dropper that drips water, while, in the New Testament, the Spirit's presence is like a pressure washer.[11]

14

MEDITATING ON SCRIPTURE

When meditation is brought up, we might think of a Buddhist monk sitting with his legs folded, trying to empty his mind. The practice of meditation, however, is not unique to Eastern religions. Meditation is prescribed by God for His people. Christians are exhorted to meditate on God's Word in order that it might sink down deep into the heart (Josh 1:8).

God breathed out the Bible so His people might know it, study it, memorize it, and love it. This requires meditation, which was the Psalmist's delight: "I will meditate on your precepts and fix my eyes on your ways" (Ps. 119:15); "Blessed is the man... [whose] delight is in the law of the LORD, and on his law he meditates day and night" (Ps. 1:2); "My eyes are awake before the watches of the night, that I may meditate on your promise" (Ps. 119:148); "I remember the days of old; I meditate on all that you have done; I ponder the work of your hands" (Ps. 143:5).

When the Bible says to "meditate," it means something different from the Buddhist approach. The Hebrew word for "meditate" is *hagah* (הגה), which can mean to "mutter," to "ponder (by talking to oneself)," or even to "read in an undertone." [1] In the Bible, meditation is an active process, unlike the Buddhists who try to empty and relax their minds. In Christian meditation, the believer is speaking and reciting, focusing on Scripture, trying to memorize it, so as to let it sink deep in the heart. We might picture a Christian walking down the street, reciting sections of the Bible or a catechism answer under his breath in meditation.

There is something supernatural about meditating on Scripture, because the Word of God is powerful (Isa 55:11; Jer 1:12; Heb 4:12). Unlike other books, studying Scripture is guided by the Holy Spirit. The Apostle Paul said, "Think over what I say, for the Lord will give you understanding in everything" (2 Tim. 2:7). Paul helps us navigate around two errors. The first error is the idea that we do not have to think because the Spirit will put understanding (unaided) in our minds. The second error is thinking the power of understanding is in our intellectual ability alone.

In 2 Timothy 2:7, notice the word "for." Paul is telling us the reason or the motivation for thinking and meditating on Scripture. We think and meditate on Scripture because "the Lord will give" us understanding. Paul is not saying that *either* we think *or* God gives understanding. Instead, Paul is saying *both* must happen: we think *and* God gives us understanding.[2] There is a special reliance upon God when we read and meditate upon Scripture.[3]

Every Christian has the Holy Spirit—the Spirit of the age to come—living inside of him or her. As we read God's Word, the Holy Spirit illumines our minds to understand.[4] This does not mean we are infallible interpreters of the Bible, but it means that the Spirit will help us by removing some of the moral blinders so that we can better understand what God wrote. We come to the Bible and we meditate on it—sometimes with much sweat and mental fatigue—knowing that the Holy Spirit is working to help us understand.

Meditation can sound taxing. Perhaps focusing on a text of Scripture for an extended period of time sounds like too much mental effort? But what else is worthy of our extended attention if not the very words of our Creator? The Scriptures are the words of eternal life (Deut 32:46-47; John 20:31); why would we not sink those words deep into our hearts? Are we seeking to love God with all of our heart, soul, mind, and strength (Mark 12:30)? Is Christ our treasure?

Obviously, we are not saved by how faithful we are in our daily Bible reading. Many Christians throughout the centuries, especially before the printing press, never owned a Bible, and many of them never learned how to read. But what does it say about our hearts when we own many copies of God's Word but never read it?[5] Think about the great privileges we have in our day with Bible apps, sermons, podcasts, and books at our fingertips.

Joel Beeke and Mark Jones write, "One hindrance to growth among Christians today is our failure to cultivate spiritual knowledge." They go on to say, "We fail to give enough time to prayer and Bible-reading, and we have abandoned the practice of meditation."[6] A lack of growth in the church is nothing new. The Apostle Paul lamented to the church at Corinth, "But I, brothers, could not address you as spiritual people, but as people of the flesh, as infants in Christ. I fed you with milk, not solid food, for you were not ready for it. And even now you are not yet ready, for you are still of the flesh" (1 Cor 3:1-3). Similarly, the writer of Hebrews rebuked the church, "For though by this time you ought to be teachers, you need someone to teach you again the basic principles of the oracles of God. You need milk, not solid food" (Heb 5:12). He exhorted them,

"Therefore let us leave the elementary doctrine of Christ and go on to maturity" (Heb 6:1).

Where we see long-term spiritual babes in Christ, we see people who have lost the practice of Christian meditation. Because head, heart, and hands are connected, when we stop meditating on biblical truths and biblical passages, our hope begins to languish and our flame dims. This was a scary outcome the Puritans knew well. Thomas Manton wrote, "Faith is lean and ready to starve unless it be fed with continual meditation on the promises (Ps 119:92)."[7] Likewise, Thomas Watson warned, "Without meditation, the truths of God will not stay with us; the heart is hard, and the memory slippery, and without meditation all is lost."[8]

Our daily routines can also spark biblical mediation. As we come across doors, vines, rooftops, and other such common items, we can immediately bring our minds to Christ and the gospel. Herman Witsius said that the "smallest object that can present itself to the eye or to the mind, will supply the richest materials" for meditation and contemplation of the perfections of God. He went on to say, "It is only necessary for us to learn to perceive in visible objects *the invisible things of God*, and to employ the creatures as ladders for ascending to the Most High God."[9] Even without an opened Bible, the book of nature is cause enough for the meditation of things divine.

Apart from growing in our knowledge and love of God, biblical mediation also brings a peace of mind to the Christian which the unbelieving world simply does not have. The Words of God are to be more desired "than gold, even much fine gold; sweeter also than honey and drippings of the honeycomb" (Ps 19:10). We should say with the Psalmist, "How sweet are your words to my taste, sweeter than honey to my mouth!" (119:103). St. Chrysostom says that the unbeliever has no hope of the future resurrection of the righteous (John 5:29; Acts 24:15). But to the Christian he says, "thou, who art travelling toward better things... hast the opportunity of meditating on the hope of the future."[10]

Unbelievers simply do not have the joys of meditating on the New Heavens and New Earth, the resurrected life, and our heavenly home with Christ. The sweet words of Scripture are like a warm blanket to the Christian pilgrim: sweet to his mouth, sweet to his heart, and sweet to his mind. May the faith that was once for all delivered to the saints be the object of our meditation (Jude 1:3).

▼

If the God-breathed Scriptures are going to be the foundation and starting place for our knowledge and thinking, then we must store them up and treasure them in our hearts. It is not enough simply to read the words of Scripture; we must meditate upon them. They are the very words of life and, as such, they are sweeter than honey to our lips. Like the Psalmist, the Christian delights in meditating on the words of God day and night. In the next chapter, we survey practical guidelines in the reading, interpretation, and applying of sacred Scripture.

> How firm a foundation, you saints of the Lord,
> is laid for your faith in his excellent Word!
> What more can he say than to you he has said,
> to you who for refuge to Jesus have fled?[11]

READING SCRIPTURE

I f we are to think God's thoughts after Him, understanding the Bible is of central importance. In this chapter, we will consider seven basic principles for reading Scripture. For a more comprehensive study on biblical interpretation, I recommend: *Reading the Word of God in the Presence of God: A Handbook for Biblical Interpretation* by Vern Poythress[1] and *Reading the Bible Supernaturally: Seeing and Savoring the Glory of God in Scripture* by John Piper.[2]

Principle One: Seek God's Meaning

The first thing to keep in mind is that God wrote the Bible. He is the primary Author, and, therefore, it is His meaning that we want to learn. We will see later that interpretation considers the human authors of Scripture, but the point needs to be made up front: We must not jettison our doctrine of Scripture in our interpretation of Scripture. God wrote the Bible and we, as readers of God's book, must seek His divine meaning.

There are occasions in Scripture when the human authors wrote higher than they knew. The words or sentences they

Principle Three: Jesus is the Focus of the Whole Bible

I once asked a group of children during Bible study, "If you were raised from the dead, what would be the first thing you'd do?" The answers varied. Some said, "I'd visit family," some said, "I'd praise God," and another said, "I'd eat a big juicy steak." The children were fascinated to discover that after Jesus rose from the dead, He had a Bible study with two disciples on the road to Emmaus. In that Bible study, Jesus showed them that the entire Old Testament was about Him, namely, His death and resurrection (Luke 24:27-48).

The apostles of Christ took this teaching to heart. Paul said that the gospel of Jesus Christ, the Son of God, was revealed in the writings of the Old Testament prophets (Rom 1:1-5; cf. Acts 26:22-23; 28:23). The gospel is not something added to the Old Testament but is intrinsic to the Old Testament. The New Testament authors did not change the Old Testament into something that it was not prior to Christ's coming in the flesh.[17] Christ and the apostles show us just how Christ-focused the Old Testament writers really were. In fact, the apostle Peter said this of the Old Testament prophets:

> Concerning this salvation, the prophets who prophesied about the grace that was to be yours searched and inquired carefully, inquiring what person or time the Spirit of Christ in them was indicating when he predicted the sufferings of Christ and the subsequent glories. *It was revealed to them that they were serving not themselves but you*, in the things that have now been announced to you through those who preached the good news to you by the Holy Spirit sent from heaven, things into which angels long to look (1 Pet 1:10-12, emphasis added).[18]

The problem with the Pharisees is that they read Moses and the prophets but missed Jesus. How can this be, when Moses and the prophets spoke about Christ? (John 5:46). Even today, many people read the Old Testament like the Pharisees. They see Israel, they see the wars, they see the laws—they see everything except Christ. If the Old Testament is about Christ, then it is dangerous to read it like a Pharisee. Lane Tipton reminds us:

> Israel, while integral to God's redemptive purpose, is from this standpoint not the paramount concern of the Old Testament Scriptures. Granted that the call of Abram, the birth of Moses, the Exodus event, the establishment of theocracy, the exile, and the restoration of God's people receive extensive attention in the Old Testament. However, all of these events subserve a more basic salvation-historical concern located in the gospel of Jesus Christ.[19]

A read through the New Testament will make evident that this was the understanding of its authors as they wrote under the inspiration of the Holy Spirit. For example, Hosea wrote, "When Israel was a child, I loved him, and out of Egypt I called my son" (Hos 11:1). Matthew interprets this as speaking about Christ (Matt 2:15). Did Matthew read something into the text that was not originally there? Or, conversely, did Hosea have Christ in view as he wrote?[20]

Again, we must remember our doctrine of Scripture. God is the primary Author of the Bible, and so we say with Abraham Kuyper: "If, therefore, it is the same Holy Spirit who spoke through the prophets and inspired the apostles, it is the same primary author who, by the apostles, *quotes himself*..."[21] Matthew understood that Hosea 1:1-11 is pointing to a future exodus and salvation from sin by the Messiah who was to come.[22]

Matthew (like Peter) understood that the Old Testament prophets spoke about Jesus.

Jesus is not only spoken of and predicted in the Old Testament (Gen 3:15; Job 9:2-4, 28-33; 16:21-22; 23:3-4; 31:35; Isa 7:14). Jesus was also depicted through *types*. David Murray defines a "type" as "a real person, place, object, or event that God ordained to act as a predictive pattern or resemblance of Jesus' person and work, or of opposition to both."[23] So, as we read the Old Testament, we will see gospel patterns and pictures of the coming Messiah. These patterns and pictures were "God ordained," meaning that they do not come from the imagination of the human reader. A type is not a manmade *allegory*; a type comes from the Author. It was perceivable by the Old Testament believers, and they were saved as they placed their faith and trust in the coming Christ.

Types in the Old Testament include the Passover lamb that taught God's people about a substitutionary sacrifice (Ex 12:13, 27; John 1:29; 1 Cor 5:7). Jonah was a type that depicted Christ's death, burial, resurrection, and the preaching of repentance (Jonah 1:15-17; Matt 12:38-41). Noah's Ark was a type, showing that only in Christ can you be saved (John 10:9; Acts 4:12; 1 Pet 3:20-22). The tabernacle was a type that depicted God's dwelling with His people in Christ (John 1:14). David, in his battle with Goliath, was a type of Christ that represented God's people in a battle against Satanic forces (Gen 3:15; 1 Sam 17:49-51; 1 John 3:8; Rev 13:3, 14). Boaz was a type that depicted Christ's redeeming capacity (Ruth 2:20; 3:9-13). Jehoiachin was a type, bearing the covenant curses in exile before being exalted (2 Kgs 24-25; Lk 24:26).[24] Examples could be multiplied.

But Jesus was not merely spoken about in prophecy and depicted in Old Testament types; He was also present with Old Testament believers. It was Jesus who led Israel out of Egypt in the Exodus event (Jude 1:5). It was Jesus who was called "the

Angel of the Lord" (Gen 16:7-13; 22:12-16; 48:15-16; Judges 6:20-24), not as a created being but as the divine representative who is identified with Yahweh.[25] Jesus Christ is Yahweh, and this truth should impact the way we read "LORD" in the Old Testament (cf. John 8:58).[26]

The Old Testament is Christian Scripture just as much as the New Testament, and its central focus is the gospel of God's Son. Jesus is spoken of in the Old Testament, communicated through types in the Old Testament, and was really present in a preincarnate form in the Old Testament.[27] Central to our interpretation of the Bible is the fact that it is about Jesus Christ and Him crucified and raised.

Principle Four: Know the Genre

God spoke in different ways: songs, poems, historical narratives, parables, wisdom literature, prophecies, letters, gospels, and apocalyptic writings. We are to keep in mind the genre being read, because each genre is not read in the same way. In order to understand the meaning of a text, we must have a good grasp on the type of genre we are reading.

"Do you take the Bible literally?", someone asked me. I knew what he meant. He was asking if I believed the Bible to be the inerrant Word of God. However, technically, I do not take the whole Bible *literally*. That is to say, I do not read a poem like I read a historical narrative, just as I do not read a grocery list like I read a love letter.

Take Habakkuk 3:19 for example: "GOD, the Lord, is my strength; he makes my feet like the deer's; he makes me tread on my high places." Does the prophet really mean that his feet supernaturally turned into deer feet? Obviously, this would be possible with God, but this is not what the prophet means to convey. Habakkuk is saying that God strengthens him and makes his feet swift (cf. 2 Sam 22:34).

In the Bible we encounter genres that are familiar to us and other genres that are completely foreign to us. For example, we modern readers have no problem with the historical accounts of Chronicles, but we struggle through the symbolic communication of Revelation.[28] For further study, consider Robert Plummer's work *Forty Questions About Interpreting the Bible,* which provides great guidelines for interpreting the different genres in Scripture.[29]

Principle Five: History Matters

When we read the Bible, we must realize that God has spoken over the course of history that has culminated in His Son, Jesus Christ. We must take *that* history into account. The writer of Hebrews began his great epistle by saying, "Long ago, at many times and in many ways, God spoke to our fathers by the prophets, but in these last days he has spoken to us by his Son" (1:1-2).

Earlier we said that, because the Bible was written by God, we must focus on the divine meaning of Scripture. But this does not mean we are unconcerned with the human authors or their historical and geographical contexts. God is Lord of history, and, as Vern Poythress teaches, "God's wisdom implies that he speaks in a way that suits the context that he himself has ordained."[30] Poythress writes elsewhere:

> Suppose a person concentrates on divine authorship. What did God intend? God intended to speak through a human author. So, rightly understood, a focus on divine authorship includes reckoning with a human author.... In speaking to Israel, God takes into account the social context in which he himself has placed them. He speaks in

Hebrew as a language that he himself has given as a gift to human beings. He speaks through a human author whom he himself has raised up.[31]

Understanding the characteristics and context of the human author can be helpful when reading Scripture. For example, knowing how Paul typically uses the word "teach" in the pastoral epistles can be helpful in understanding how he is using the word in 1 Timothy 2:12.[32] Knowing the historical background of a passage can also prove helpful. Without knowing the background of the Jewish and Samaritan relationship, one might miss the point of Luke 10:25-37.[33] Moreover, knowing something of the geographical context will aid in understanding passages like Revelation 3:15-16.[34]

Nevertheless, we must affirm that the background of the New Testament is the Old Testament,[35] and that, while knowing the historical context can be beneficial in *illuminating* some details, it can never be *determinative*.[36] The Bible is a cohesive unit; it is clear and sufficient. One does not have to be a historian to understand the Bible; the Christian is not chained to extra-biblical (i.e., outside the Bible) documents and writings in order to rightly understand and interpret Scripture.

Principle Six: Ask Good Questions

One of the best ways to gain greater understanding of Scripture is to ask good questions. Come to a text of Scripture and riddle it with questions. Once we have probed and queried the text, we seek out answers to those questions using other Scripture passages, Study Bibles, maps of the area, lexicons, concordances, Bible dictionaries, commentaries, as well as resources in biblical, systematic, and historical theology.

Let us use Romans 16:7 as an example: "Greet Andronicus and Junia, my kinsmen and my fellow prisoners. They are well known to the apostles, and they were in Christ before me." If we want to understand this text better, we might ask a series of questions like this:

- Who is the author?
- Who is the audience?
- What do we know about the area or city that is receiving this letter?
- What is the surrounding context of this passage?
- How does it add to the author's argument or purpose for chapter 16?
- Chapter 16 began with the conjunction δὲ; does this say anything about the relationship between chapters 15-16?
- What do we know about Andronicus and Junia?
- When Paul says "fellow prisoners," does he mean that they are "slaves of Christ" metaphorically, or are they actually sitting in a prison cell?
- How does Paul typically use the word "prisoner"?
- The Greek word for "well known" is ἐπίσημοι; what are some other possible meanings of this word?
- What does it mean to be "in Christ"?
- There seems to be a sense in which a believer was "in Christ" before creation (Eph 1:4-6) and also "in Christ" when Jesus died and rose from the dead (Rom 6:4, 8; 2 Tim 2:11). How do all of these texts shape how we understand being "in Christ"?
- Are there any Old Testament texts that speak of being "in God" or "in the Lord"?
- Is there a difference between being "in Christ" and Christ being "with us"?

- How have the historic creeds and confessions of the church used Romans 16:7?

These are some of the questions we could ask a text like Romans 16:7. Some of them might yield little or no fruit, and others might open vistas that we were not expecting. The key to seeing the richness of Scripture is to ask good questions. It is amazing the things we will see in the Bible if we slow down, look at the text, and ask questions.

Another query might be: How does a particular truth in Scripture develop or progress throughout the Bible? For this, Reference Bibles come in handy. They usually have a column down the middle of the page or off to the side with citations of other Scripture passages that relate to the text being read. Suppose one is reading a text that is speaking about grumbling and would like to trace passages about grumbling from Genesis onward. Perhaps it would look something like this: Genesis 3:12 →
Exodus 15:24; 16:1-2; 17:3 → Numbers 16:41, 46; 17:5 → Joshua 9:18
→ Matthew 20:11 → 1 Corinthians 10:10 → Philippians 2:14 → 1
Peter 4:9. Tracing this theme throughout the Bible may help us discern more clearly what grumbling is and why it is so offensive to God.

The point of asking good questions, of course, is to find the Author's main point.[37] What is He trying to teach us? It often helps to trace the flow of the Author's argument or idea. In order to do this, it helps to keep an eye on the connecting words. Those small words to which we often pay no attention can actually tell us a lot: words like "for," "likewise," "so that," or "therefore." Keep an eye on those words and ask, "How do these sentences or paragraphs relate to each other?"[38] As you see the flow of the Author's thought, you begin to see the meaning—or the main point—that God intended.

Principle Seven: Application is Rooted in Meaning

"What does this passage mean to you?" This is a common question heard in small groups and Bible studies. The question, however, is a bad one. It presupposes that the text is a lump of clay that can be molded to fit anyone's liking. The reader does not determine the meaning of the text; the Author determines the meaning of the text. In order to apply a text to your life situation, you must first find the Author's original meaning. The application may change with the person, culture, and time period, but the meaning will never change.

When personal application is rooted in the objective meaning of a passage, there is an increased confidence in the application. The application will warm the heart more if it is rooted in the actual meaning of the passage. John Piper wrote that "the power of that application will increase with the confidence that it is based on real, objective, unchanging meaning that is really there."[39]

But what about the 'odd' parts of the Old Testament? The Old Testament is filled with wars, kings, sacrifices, dietary and cleanliness laws, and so forth. This is where Edmund Clowney's famous diagram[40] proves helpful:

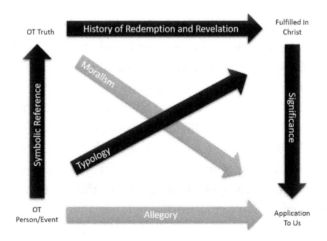

Let us use the well-known account of David and Goliath as our Old Testament event (1 Sam 16-17). It would be a mistake to go from event to application without first discovering the truth being conveyed. Someone may allegorize the text and say something like, "David chose five stones corresponding to the five types of sacrifices found in Leviticus 1-7, because David's victory was going to be a pleasing aroma to God." But this comes from the creative mind of the reader, not the Author. Allegorizing happens when someone picks something in the text and gives it "an interpretation that is unrelated to the context or meaning."[41]

Instead of allegorizing the text, we must determine the Old Testament truth being conveyed in the event. The Book of Judges left God's people longing for a king, and the books of Ruth and Samuel show us that the needed king is David. He is the anointed, Holy Spirit-filled representative of God's people who will not hear the blasphemies of Goliath and stand by idle. The fate of God's people rests upon his victory alone.[42]

But here one can make another wrong turn down the *moralistic* road by going directly to application and saying things like, "David defeated his giant, and we can defeat our giants as well if we just believe like David." This, however, moves to application too hastily and flattens this great historical account into mere moral principles.

The battle between David and Goliath points us to the battle between Christ and Satan (Gen 3:15; 1 John 3:8; Rev 12:1-6). David is a type of Christ, and Goliath, with his scaly armor (1 Sam 17:5), is a type of Satan. Clowney draws out this comparison: "Jesus Christ, the Messiah... meets and conquers Satan the strong man so that he may deliver those who are Satan's captives (Luke 11:15-19)."[43]

Having gone through all the proper steps, what is a good application of this text? Where are *we* in this text? We are like the Israelites on the sidelines watching this great battle, rejoicing in our covenant representative as he fights on our behalf.[44] We are not David slaying the spiritual giants that plague us. Christ, the greater David, has fought and won on our behalf. We have victory over our spiritual giants only if we are united to Christ by the Spirit and through faith, for it is Christ who has bound the strong man and liberated the captives. Christ is victorious and, in Christ, we too are victorious.[45]

———————▼———————

In this chapter, we have surveyed various principles, guidelines, and steps for faithfully reading Scripture. If we have any hope of properly meditating on God's Word and thinking His thoughts after Him, we must properly understand what He says. Far too often, a reader inserts his or her own meaning into the text. When this happens, the reader is not thinking God's thoughts after Him. God has written and preserved Scripture for us and has given us the Holy Spirit to help us understand it. Faithful Christians may still disagree on various parts, but it is a sin against God to treat the Bible as if it were too opaque, too convoluted, or too complex to be understood by the average Christian. Let us grow in our ability to interpret the Bible so we can hear Christ's voice more clearly and follow Him more faithfully. In the next chapter, we explore various ways in which we can study and examine God's Word.

> Eternal is your word, O Lord;
> in heav'n it stands forever sure.
> Your truth remains thro' every age:
> the earth you founded, it endures.
> They stand by your decree this day,
> for all things serve your sov'reign way.[46]

WAYS OF STUDYING GOD'S WORD

Charles Hodge defined theology as "the science of the facts of divine revelation so far as those facts concern the nature of God and our relation to him, as his creatures, as sinners, and as the subjects of redemption."[1] But there are different types of theology or ways of doing theology. Geerhardus Vos speaks of the *theological encyclopedia*.[2] In this chapter, we will learn about the five "departments" of theology and how they relate to one another: Exegetical Theology, Biblical Theology, Systematic Theology, Historical Theology, and Practical Theology.

Exegetical Theology

In the title "Exegetical Theology" (ET),[3] we have a form of the word *exegesis*, which is the interpretation and examination of individual passages of Scripture.[4] In ET, we zoom in and consider a single passage or a narrow group of passages. There are resources available to help us search Greek and Hebrew words as well as gain insight into the text's syntax and grammar. ET also considers differences among the manuscripts (i.e., copies of Scripture that occasionally contain minor differences). For example, is Matthew 17:21 original to Matthew's Gospel, or should it be left out? Should Mark 9:29 say "prayer and fasting" or just "prayer"? Can the most reliable and oldest manuscripts shed light on these texts? Though these differences do not affect any major doctrines, they *do* occasionally affect the nuance of our interpretation of a particular passage.

Biblical Theology

The discipline of Biblical Theology (BT)[5] studies the history of special revelation.[6] This type of study is concerned with how the narrative of redemption organically "unfolds" throughout covenant history.[7] Guy Water explained, "Biblical revelation is *progressive* in that it moves toward a divinely predetermined goal, namely, the person and work of Jesus Christ. Biblical revelation is *organic* in that this movement resembles the growth of an organism." Scripture is divine commentary on God's mighty deeds of creation and redemption. BT traces the progression of this revelation, exploring how God's self-revelation in the Bible has unfolded from Genesis to Revelation.

Doing BT, one might trace themes that unfold from Genesis to Revelation (themes of clothing, kingdom, wilderness, offspring, and so on).[8] One might even compare, for example, what the Pentateuch says about a topic with what the Gospels say about that topic, in order to see how God's revelation on that particular topic has progressed throughout redemptive history. Additionally, one might consider the theology of a single biblical author on one particular topic and ask something like, What is Paul's theology of atonement?

Systematic Theology

Instead of interpreting a single passage, the department of Systematic Theology (ST)[9] asks "whole-Bible" questions. For example, one might ask, What does the Bible say about prayer? or, What does the Bible teach us about the birth of Christ? To answer questions like these, one would bring all the relevant texts together (read and understood in their proper contexts) in order to understand the Bible's whole teaching on that particular doctrine. ST organizes and gives detailed summaries of the important topics in theology.[10] The difference between BT and ST, says Vos, is that "Biblical Theology draws a *line* of development. Systematic Theology draws a *circle*."[11] ST approaches the Bible as a *completed, united,* and *sufficient* canon of God's revelation.

Further, ST is a nonspeculative discipline that is concerned with what "is either expressly set down in Scripture, or by good and necessary consequence may be deduced from Scripture" (Westminster Confession of Faith 1.6).[12] An example of a "good and necessary consequence" would be the hypostatic union of Jesus, which is the doctrine that God the Son incarnate is one *Person* with two *natures*—one fully and only human (yet without sin), and the other fully and only divine. These natures are "without confusion, without change, without division, without separation."[13] Though the Bible never explains the person of Christ in these exact terms, they reflect what the Bible *does* say about the incarnation of God the Son, and we recognize this when all the relevant passages are brought together and their implications considered. This was first articulated in this language at the Council of Chalcedon, bringing us to our next "department" of theology.

3:16). Creeds and confessions form a "pattern of sound words" to which we are to hold fast (2 Tim 1:13).

Practical Theology

Finally, Practical Theology (PT)[21] is concerned with taking what is learned from ET, BT, ST, and HT and then applying it to the life of the individual Christian and the church. PT is concerned with the appropriate practice of things like preaching, biblical counseling, liturgy, leadership, discipleship, evangelism, and Christian living. The doctrines of Scripture must be proclaimed and heralded, they must be applied to embattled sheep, and they must inform our life and worship.

PT helps pastors, for example, think through the mission of the church. Christ has given the church both the method and the message to make disciples of all nations (Mat 28:18-20; Acts 2:41-42).[22] The times in which we live are constantly changing, but the gospel remains the same (Isa 40:8). Regardless of the decade or the century, humans still need Christ for the forgiveness of sins. The pastor will endeavor to speak persuasively to his audience but will never compromise on the gospel. The Word, sacraments, and prayer remain the marching orders of Christ's church until He returns.

Now that we have seen the various departments of theology, the question that remains is, How do they relate? Is it the case that we first do ET, then move on to BT, then ST, and so forth, in a pyramid fashion? I believe that it is better to see a mutual relationship between each "department" of theology. As we do ST, we keep BT and ET in our peripheral vision and allow those other disciplines to help us. As we do ST, BT, and ET, we let HT set the boundaries. All theology (if it is sound) is practical, and so we bring the fruit of all these theologies to aid the church in her worship, life, and mission. The diagram[23] below illustrates how we ought to view the relationship between the various theologies:

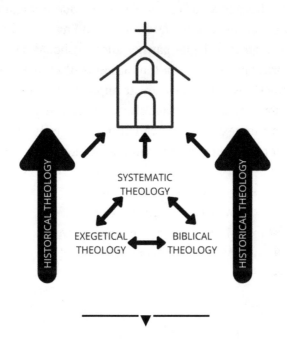

As the Christian reads and studies the Bible, it is helpful to keep in mind the various ways in which one can carry this out. The Christian will certainly seek to unpack the various texts of Scripture and also keep an eye toward the unfolding storyline of the Bible. Because the Bible is a closed canon and sufficient for life and godliness, we can approach Scripture and ask the whole Bible questions about any one of its topics. ET, BT, and ST have a reciprocal relationship in which they are constantly and mutually informing one another. As the Christian focuses on ET, he brings with him (in his peripheral vision) the fruits of BT and ST; when the Christian focuses on BT, he brings with him the fruits of ET and ST, and so on.[24] Moreover, the Christian should not be a hyper-individualist, believing it is all about "me and my Bible." The Christian knows that the Holy Spirit has been with the Church for thousands of years. While creeds and confessions are subordinate to Scripture, they provide summaries and boundaries for our reading and understanding of God's Word. History is a great dialogue partner and we should be eager to find historical precedence for the various truths that we believe. Finally, the Christian studies how to apply the fruit of these disciplines not only to his life but also to his ministry in the local church. In the next chapter, we consider the context or background for our reading of and thinking through Scripture.

Holy Bible, book divine,
Precious treasure, thou art mine;
Mine to tell me whence I came;
Mine to teach me what I am.[25]

THE CONTEXT OF THINKING

I n Bible College, I can remember sitting next to a person who did not attend church. I was perplexed about this. Here we were, preparing for the ministry, learning Systematic Theology, hearing great lectures, and for him all this was *disconnected* from the local church. How could this be? How could these truths be learned, loved, and lived in a vacuum? Do these truths not lead one to worship God, fellowship with other believers, and serve the local church?

In this chapter, I unpack the context required for our reading and thinking. We cannot read, study, and meditate in an environment or context that is antithetical or contrary to God and then expect to grow in the way that God intends. Our reading of and thinking through the Bible must be done in a God-ordained context. Below I explain what this context looks like for the child and the Christian.

The Child's Context

The context for a child, most basically, is a loving, Christ-saturated home where he or she is provided for (1 Tim 5:8) and

encouraged (Col 3:21). The Apostle Paul wrote, "Fathers, do not
provoke your children to anger, but bring them up in the discipline and instruction of the Lord" (Eph 6:4). Anger gives the
devil a foothold (Eph 4:26-27), and so the father must promote a
Christ-like peace and stability in the home. He does this by disciplining and instructing according to the Lord. Let us look at
each of these individually.

God has much to say about how we are to discipline the
children He has given us.[1] After all, our children ultimately belong to God, and we are called to be good stewards, following
God in the raising of *His* children. Here are some statements
God has made about corrective discipline:

> Whoever heeds instruction is on the path to life, but he
> who rejects reproof leads others astray. (Proverbs 10:17)

> Whoever spares the rod hates his son, but he who loves
> him is diligent to discipline him. (Proverbs 13:24)

> Folly is bound up in the heart of a child, but the rod of
> discipline drives it far from him. (Proverbs 22:15)

> Do not withhold discipline from a child; if you strike
> him with a rod, he will not die. If you strike him with
> the rod, you will save his soul from Sheol. (Proverbs
> 23:13-14)

> The rod and reproof give wisdom, but a child left to him-
> self brings shame to his mother. (Proverbs 29:15)

> Discipline your son, and he will give you rest; he will give
> delight to your heart. (Proverbs 29:17)

Perhaps images of a drunken father beating and abusing his children came to mind when you read the above Scriptures. But that image has nothing to do with the discipline God is prescribing for parents. Tedd Tripp explains: "Use of the rod is not a matter of an angry parent venting his wrath upon a small, helpless child. The use of the rod signifies a faithful parent recognizing his child's dangerous state and employing a God-given remedy."[2] The word "rod" denotes a "stick or rod used for correction or punishment."[3] It certainly is not a torturing device. Today, when we hear "rod," we think of a curtain or shower rod. It was certainly not that big or weighty. While some measured use of a "rod" can be helpful when correcting *your* child, spanking may be done with an opened hand (especially when children are small).

According to God, the "rod" (שֵׁבֶט) is for those lacking biblical wisdom (Prov 10:13) and exhibiting folly (Prov 22:15; 26:3). Folly occurs, to give one example, when one disobeys parental instruction (Prov 1:7-9; 2:20-23; 23:22-26). The rod is a rescuing device, liberating the child from the path that leads to Hell (Prov 10:17; 23:14).[4] The rod also imparts wisdom (Prov 29:15) and removes folly from the heart (Prov 22:15). Therefore, parents must not withhold the rod (Prov 23:13) but be diligent in its use (Prov 13:24).

Ultimately, our children belong to God, and He has tasked us to be good stewards of His children. This includes using the rod appropriately and biblically on His behalf.[5] Joel Beeke says, "The goal is not to reduce each child to a puddle of quivering fear and abject passivity, but to bring him to the point of acknowledging that his father and mother are the rulers in the home and he is to stand in awe before his parents, showing them deep respect and submitting to their God-given authority."[6] He goes on to give this practical advice:

> Angry discipline is counterproductive as a means of train-
> ing our children in godliness.... So, we should pray before
> applying the rod: "Lord, quench all my anger, fill me with
> love for this child, and let me punish him with compas-
> sion and the desire to do him good. Keep me from being
> an Eli who fails to discipline, but also keep me from the
> error of Saul, who lashed out at his own son in murderous
> rage" (see 1 Sam. 3:13; 14:43-44) .... We should take the
> child into a room away from the family, explain what we
> are about to do and why we must do it, then administer
> the punishment. Afterwards, we should take the child in
> our arms, tell him we love him, and pray with him. We
> ought to take as much time as needed to say and do all
> we can to restore a right relationship with him.[7]

Discipline cannot be divorced from instruction. Fathers are
to bring their children up in both the *discipline* and *instruction*
of the Lord. As the rod of discipline is driving out the anti-God
folly from the child's heart (Ps 14:1), the parents are instructing
the child in the ways of Christ and filling his or her mind and
heart with Scriptural truths and promises from God (Ps 78).

As the child grows and develops a worldview, he or she is sitting upon a three-legged stool. One leg is the home, the second
is the church, and the third is the school. The home, church, and
school ought to be united in their theological outlook and in
their focus on Christ. As Richard Baxter wrote, "Theology must
lay the foundation, and lead the way of all our studies."[8] If one of
these three "legs" is missing or promoting a worldview contrary
to the biblical worldview, the other two legs will have to bear
more weight.

In the Old Testament, God commanded parents to take every opportunity to teach their children. He commands His people

to talk about His words "when you are sitting in your house, and when you are walking by the way, and when you lie down, and when you rise" (Deut 11:19). This parental mandate has not been relaxed in the New Testament, for parents are always to instruct their children diligently. Divine, spiritual, and saving truth, says G. H. Gerberding, "is not in man by nature... It must be put into man before he can have it."[9] This is done with regular family worship, reading Scripture and other Christian books before bed, diligent catechization, and faithful church attendance.[10]

Faithful church attendance every Lord's Day will show a child that church is the high point of the week. This is one of the chief ways that our children are instructed and one of the chief contexts in which our children will develop a biblical worldview. In Nehemiah 8, Ezra is gathering God's people in order to read from the law, and he read it, we are told, "in the presence of the men and the women and those who could understand" (8:3). Who are "those who could understand"? Those are the children. Many children between the ages of five and eight could be classified as "those who could understand." These children gathered with their fathers and mothers to hear the Scriptures read and then explained (8:8), and they did so with attentive ears (8:3).

Let your child see how excited you are on the Lord's Day to meet and commune with Christ through Word and sacrament. Far too often, we convey the opposite to our children. We approach church like it is a boring duty, something to endure. We show up nearly lifeless. Other times, we approach church like a grumpy old Pharisee, focusing on side issues or lobbying for our personal preferences, all the while missing Christ. Let us, rather, show our children that we have a child-like faith and a child-like desire to fellowship with Christ and serve others.

For children, the context for learning the Scriptures and developing a biblical worldview is a loving home where discipline drives out folly, where the parents teach diligently, and where church is a highlight of the week. The home, the church, and the school all bear the responsibility of instructing the children that God has given us.[11] In this environment, the child can begin to think God's thoughts after Him, using his or her mind and living a life that brings Christ glory. In time, we pray that the child will be saved and place his or her faith and trust in the Lord Jesus Christ. Then, he or she will come to the Bible with a heart that fears God and with a life that has a regular rhythm of worship with other believers in the local church. This hope brings us to our next section.

The Christian's Internal Context

Proper reading of and thinking through Scripture cannot take place within a dead heart. The individual Christian's heart and mind is his or her *internal* context of thinking. Solomon tells us, "The fear of the LORD is the beginning of wisdom, and the knowledge of the Holy One is insight" (Prov 9:10). True wisdom and knowledge comes from a heart that fears God (unlike worldly wisdom; James 3:13-18).[12] Bruce Waltke gives a helpful analogy: "What the alphabet is to reading, notes to reading music, and numerals to mathematics, the fear of the LORD is to attaining" godly wisdom.[13]

Jesus Himself said, "And do not fear those who kill the body but cannot kill the soul. Rather fear him who can destroy both soul and body in hell" (Matt 10:28). It is proper for the people of God to have a healthy fear of Him. Polycarp, church father and disciple of the apostle John, impressed the fear of God upon his readers, saying, "[W]e are before the eyes of our Lord and God, and 'we must all appear at the judgment-seat of Christ, and must every one give an account of himself.' Let us then serve Him in fear, and with all reverence..."[14]

Fear of the Lord is not the same as *terror* of the Lord (Isa 2:19). The terror of the Lord happens when the wicked are about to receive the just wrath of the Almighty God and they beg for rocks to crush them instead (Heb 10:31; Rev 6:15-17). God's people are His beloved children, which means that we should not have a slavish terror or dread of God.

The fear of the Lord is a *reverential* fear and *awe* of God. It is a deep respect akin to the respect a child exhibits toward his loving and just father. When you fear God, you fear offending Him, and so you submit to Him and His will for all things (Job 31:23; Ps 36:1-4; Eccl 12:13).[15] God is a loving Father, working all things for our good in Christ (Rom 8:28-29), which includes disciplining us for holiness (1 Thess 4:3-8; Heb 12:7-13).

Without a heart-context of love, trust, and fear, your reading of and thinking through Scripture will be fruitless. God says that wisdom must come from a foundation that fears Him. Without the fear of the Lord, there can be no godly wisdom.

The Christian's External Context

Just as there is an *internal* context for Christian thinking, there is also an *external* context. The proper external context for the Christian as he reads and thinks through Scripture is one in which he is involved in a local church and connected to the corporate life of God's people. Too often, especially in the West, we tend to have a low view of church and a high view of the individual. This order, however, must be reversed. "The church at worship," writes Nicolas Alford, "is the epicenter of our spiritual lives, and of God's program for His people on earth."[16]

Unlike modern thinking, the Bible speaks of the church in glorious ways. The church is the "bride" of Christ (Rev 19:7-9), is being built and protected by Christ (Matt 16:16-19), is being nourished by Christ (Eph 5:22-33), is being led by Christ (Col 1:18), and is the very "household" of God (1 Tim 3:15). Even the angels cannot help but to stand in awe as they behold the manifold wisdom of God on display in and through the church (Eph 3:7-13). Peter's description of the church is breathtaking: "But you are a chosen race, a royal priesthood, a holy nation, a people for his own possession, that you may proclaim the excellencies of him who called you out of darkness into his marvelous light" (1 Pet 2:9-10). It's no wonder John Calvin wrote, "For those to whom he [God] is Father the church may also be mother."[17] And, likewise, Jonathan Leeman, "There's nothing on earth like the local church—it comes from the end of time!"[18]

If the Christian is to grow and mature, there are three important contextual elements needed to foster and support that growth: liturgy, the ordinary means of grace, and pastoral care. We consider each one in turn:

Element One: Liturgy

The word "liturgy" simply refers to what the people of God do when they worship. The elements and order of our Sunday worship is our liturgy. The church bulletin will often display the *order of worship* for that particular church. Every single church has a liturgy; the only question is if a church has a biblically regulated liturgy that is well thought out and appropriately executed.[19]

As G. K. Beale warned, we become what we worship.[20] If we are to think God's thoughts after Him, we must worship Him. How can we think properly if we are becoming more like a false god? Everyone worships something; humans are created to be worshipers. But are we worshiping the one, true, and living God or an idol? The worship of God is of central importance not only to the individual Christian but also for the entire church. Alford writes, "The church's task of worship is not easily undertaken, but it is easily the most important task she undertakes. Thus it behooves all Christians to think deeply and search diligently the Scriptures to see how God would have us proceed."[21] God has told His church, in the Bible, how He wants to be worshiped; we are not permitted to be inventive or innovative, lest we wander into idolatry.[22]

So, why is it important to have a good, biblical liturgy to order our Sunday service? The ancient saying captures the reason: *lex orandi, lex credendi* ("The rule of worship is the rule of faith").[23] Jordan Cooper explains: "In other words, worship and belief are intimately connected: how we worship impacts what we believe, and what we believe impacts how we worship."[24] Every element of our worship is shaping and reinforcing what we believe about God, ourselves, and our world.

Each Lord's Day, Christ's people gather to worship the Triune God in Spirit and in truth, with reverence and awe.[25] As we worship, the communion between God and His people is strengthened and made to grow. There is a healthy rhythm in our worship week after week that reaffirms and shapes what we believe. God is not only praised, but His people are, in a way, catechized by the liturgy.[26]

As the people of God gather for worship, there is a dialogue between God and His covenant people, a back and forth where God initiates and we respond—a kind of holy conversation or transaction (Ex 19-24; Josh 24:14-28; Neh 8:2-9; Rev 4-5).[27] Our liturgy reminds us that *we* do not "do church." *God* "does church." Worship is ultimately "top down."[28] God creates a community of sinners washed by the blood of His Son and He fills them with praise, thanksgiving, and love (Ps 40:3). God gathers us, God protects us, God instructs us, and God nourishes us. It is all of grace! The only reason we gather as a church body is because of God.[29] An example liturgy that displays this dialogue principle might look something like this:

> Call to Worship
> Invocation and Prayer of Praise
> Psalm[30] or Hymn of Praise
> Responsive Reading of the Ten Commandments
> Confession of Sin
> Psalm or Hymn of Repentance
> Assurance of Pardon
> Psalm or Hymn of Thanksgiving
> Prayer of Illumination
> Scripture Reading
> Prayer for Offering
> Collection of Offering
> Psalm or Hymn
> Preaching of the Word
> Prayer of Intercession and the Lord's Prayer
> Apostles' Creed
> The Lord's Supper
> Closing Doxology
> Benediction[31]

In the sample liturgy above, we begin with a call to worship (Ex 5:1; 24:1; Ps 29:2). God is summoning His people to worship Him on the Lord's Day: "Hallelujah! Praise God in his sanctuary. Praise him in his mighty expanse. Praise him for his powerful acts; praise him for his abundant greatness" (Ps 150:1-2, CSB).

"Our gathering, our songs, our sermons, our fellowship around the table," writes Mike Cosper, "is a response to his initiation and invitation."[32]

Flowing from this call, the worshiping church follows a gospel pattern. We call upon the name of the Lord in the invocation (Ps 8:1; 67:1-3). The Law then shows us God's perfect standard and our own sinfulness (Ex 24:5-6; Gal 3:10). Subsequently, we are driven to Christ for forgiveness (Rom 8:1, 33; 1 John 1:9). We hear the Word both read and proclaimed (Neh 8:8; 2 Tim 3:16; Heb 4:12). We confess our historic faith together in the Apostles' Creed or Nicene Creed. We see the Word made visible in the sacraments. God's ordained minister proclaims a blessing upon the flock as they depart (Luke 24:50; Heb 13:20-21; Jude 1:24-25).[33]

Scattered throughout the Divine Service are songs of praise where the saints join their voices with instrumental accompaniment in adoration for who God is and what God has done (Ps 100:1-2). We sing of God saving us: "Jesus sought me when a stranger, wandering from the fold of God."[34] We sing of the splendor and beauty of God: "Immortal, invisible, God only wise, in light inaccessible hid from our eyes."[35] And we sing of our response to God: "Nothing in my hands I bring, simply to the cross I cling."[36]

Imagine how a life of faith and biblical thinking can be fostered and caused to grow in a weekly liturgical worship rhythm where the believer gathers with other redeemed saints to sing praises to the Triune God (Ps 65:1), to recite the Ten Commandments, Lord's Prayer, and Apostles' Creed, and to feed upon Christ through Word and sacrament. A church with a good, biblical liturgy is an absolute must for a proper external context in which to read and think about Scripture. David Rueter said it well:

In worship, the liturgy of the Church teaches believers, new and old, the language of our relationship with God and one another. Through our worship, we come to learn the story of the relationship between God and His creation, the fall and subsequent redemption through Christ. In worship, Christ comes to us through Word and Sacrament.[37]

Element Two: The Ordinary Means of Grace

Even though Christ ascended into Heaven (Acts 1:9), believers on earth are still united to Christ by the Holy Spirit and through faith (Gal 2:20; 1 John 1:3). In fact, Christ is constantly interceding for His people at the right hand of God the Father (Heb 7:25; 1 John 2:1).[38] Christ is the head of His church (Col 1:18) and He continues to bestow grace and blessings to His church.[39]

Ephesians 1:3 teaches that God the Father is to be praised because He, through the ministry of the Holy Spirit, brings redemptive grace, which Christ has purchased for us, to our souls (see John 16:14).[40] Through the Spirit, Christ "nourishes and cherishes" the church (Eph 5:29), which He bought with His own blood (Acts 20:28). Carl Trueman said it well: "The church has a real, visible, material existence, and it is the place where God works out his purposes both corporately and for individuals. It is where Christ is to be found, where he rules people, where he nurtures them, and where he brings them to spiritual maturity."[41] Trueman went on to say, "[T]he primary reason we go to church is to receive God's grace through word and sacraments."[42]

How can we understand this grace that God bestows upon Christ's Church? Let us begin by first defining the phrase "ordinary means of grace." Once we have a working definition, we can explore what are the means of grace. And finally, we will consider what is meant by "ordinary." For a definition of a "means of grace," Richard Barcellos captures all the proper elements: a means of grace is

> the delivery systems God has instituted to bring grace—that is, spiritual power, spiritual change, spiritual help, spiritual fortitude, spiritual blessings—to needy souls on the earth. Grace comes from our Father, through the Son, by the Spirit ordinarily in conjunction with the ordained means. The means of grace are those conduits through which Christ alters, modifies, adjusts, changes, transforms, and develops souls on the earth. Herman Bavinck says, 'Christ is and remains the acquisitor as well as the distributor of grace.' That is, Christ acquired grace *for* us and distributed grace *to* or *in* us. In order to get acquired grace *to* or *in* us, God ordained means through which it is distributed. The means of grace, then, are God's delivery system through which that which was acquired *for* us gets distributed or delivered *to* or *in* us.[43]

A means of grace could be compared to a military supply drop. God has told us the time and coordinates for this supply drop, namely, on the Lord's Day at a local church where the Word is faithfully preached and the sacraments are faithfully administered.[44] As we gather on the Lord's Day with God's redeemed people, Christ communicates or imparts to us the benefits of redemption.[45]

If this is what a means of grace *is*, what *are* these means? They are the Word, the sacraments, and prayer. The Word is primary, because it is the means by which God calls His elect into a life of faith, as well as the means by which the elect are nourished and sustained. How will sinners come to faith in a God they have never known? "Faith comes from hearing, and hearing through the word of Christ" (Rom 10:17).

The Word is the means by which the elect are called and also the means by which the elect are sustained and nourished. The preaching of the Word week after week is a means by which Christ is present with His people, speaking to them the words of life.[46] When a local covenant community of believers gathers on the Lord's Day to hear the Word preached, they should expect to hear the "voice" of Christ, coming through the faithful preaching of Scripture. When the Word is accurately and faithfully expounded, the congregation is hearing the Word of God proclaimed. As the Second Helvetic Confession affirms:

> THE PREACHING OF THE WORD OF GOD IS THE WORD OF GOD. Wherefore when this Word of God is now preached in the church by preachers lawfully called, we believe that the very Word of God is proclaimed, and received by the faithful; and that neither any other Word of God is to be invented nor is to be expected from heaven: and that now the Word itself which is preached is to be regarded, not the minister that preaches; for even if he be evil and a sinner, nevertheless the Word of God remains still true and good.[47]

Some people fret that they cannot remember every sermon they hear. "How can I grow as a Christian, if I can't remember the sermon from two weeks ago?", they might ask. It is helpful to remember how learning rewires our brains. We do not remember each and every reading class we had in elementary school, but when we pick up a book, we can read the words on each page.[48] Similarly, while we do not remember each and every sermon we have ever heard, those sermons have rewired our brains so that, as we go about our daily lives, we interpret the world through the lens of Scripture and make decisions that bring glory to Christ. Trueman said, "It is the slow, incremental impact of sitting under the Word week by week, and year by year, that makes the difference. That is how we mature as Christians."[49]

After the Word are the sacraments.[50] Hercules Collins, a 17th-century Baptist, defined *sacraments* as "sacred signs and seals set before our eyes and ordained of God for this purpose, that He may declare and confirm by them the promise of His gospel unto us, to this, that He gives freely remission of sins and life everlasting to everyone in particular who believes in the sacrifice of Christ which He accomplished once for all upon the cross."[51]

The sacraments, according to Scripture, are Baptism and the Lord's Supper (*Eucharist*). God ordained that the church observe these two sacraments so that believers would understand gospel truths more clearly, have reassurance of gospel promises, and receive gospel graces.[52] The sacraments are the visible Word whereby they comfort the conscience of a believer, sealing Christ and all His benefits to his or her heart. Believers, on their part, confess and confirm their faith in and love for God in partaking of the sacraments.[53]

The Baptist Catechism teaches that Baptism and the Lord's Supper are "effectual means of salvation, not for any virtue in them, or in him that doth administer them, but only by the blessing of Christ, and the working of the Spirit in those that by faith receive them."[54] It must be remembered that Scripture speaks about salvation as a past, present, and future reality. A believer *has been* saved (Eph 2:8-9), *is being* saved (1 Cor 1:18), and *will be* saved (Rom 5:9). This particular catechism question and answer is speaking about the ongoing, continuing process of being saved and nourished by Christ.[55]

The sacraments give comfort to the conscience and press upon us the reality which they signify: that Christ has removed our sins and washed us whiter than snow (Acts 22:16).[56] Notice what the catechism stated: it is the presence of Christ, the working of the Spirit, and the faith of the partaker that make the sacrament effectual, not the elements themselves or the holiness of the minister administering the sacrament.[57] As John Calvin said, "If the Spirit be lacking, the sacraments can accomplish nothing more in our minds than the splendor of the sun shining upon blind eyes, or a voice sounding in deaf ears."[58] We must remember that the main "direction" in the sacraments is *from* God *to* His church, working in and through the faithful by the power of the Holy Spirit (1 Cor 10:16).

As signs and seals, the sacraments both signify and confirm to us the salvation purchased by Christ. The sacraments bring these invisible, spiritual realities to mind and they also validate, confirm, and attest to the truthfulness of these realities.[59] They are not merely pictures but *notarized* pictures, notarized by the King of kings and Lord of lords. Like an official wax seal upon a king's letter, baptism and the Lord's Supper seal to us the promises of God put forth in Christ Jesus, assuring us that God's promises can be trusted.[60]

As with the preaching of the Word and prayer (1 Tim 2:1; 4:13, 16; James 5:16), the sacraments are not only commanded by Christ (Matt 28:19; Luke 22:19); they are commands that come with the promise that Christ will work through them (Matt 28:20; Mark 16:16; Luke 22:20; Acts 2:38).[61] As Thomas Vincent put it, "When the minister doth give forth the sign or outward elements, in the sacramental action, the Lord doth give forth and convey the things signified [i.e., the benefits of the new covenant] unto the worthy receivers."[62]

Just as Christ is wholly present to us in the Word, so too in the sacraments Christ is wholly present to us as our eyes of faith are brought to Heaven where Christ is seated.[63] The Sacraments serve to strengthen our faith; they are God's means to nourish us with the redemption purchased by Christ.[64] Food and water nourish our physical bodies, and Word and sacrament nourish our spiritual bodies. In fact, Vos warns, "Not making use of the sacrament must impoverish spiritual life and cause it to deteriorate." [65]

However, we should not think that Christ is absent six days of the week and only appears on the Lord's Day, for Christ is always with us. Nevertheless, when a believer takes the sacrament by faith, Christ is "ever more intimately united" to him or her.[66] As Vos said, though fellowship with Christ is never completely broken off, there are times when it is "especially strengthened." [67] This strengthening of our faith comes through the ordinary means of grace. The "Spirit of God brings soul-nourishing and faith-strengthening blessings from heaven to Christ's people on the earth by the blessing of God," write Barcellos.[68]

Baptism is something the Christian should remember again and again throughout his or her pilgrimage. When we are tempted, when we are weary, or when the devil oppresses us, our baptism ought to provide for us sweet reflection and assurance because of the reality it signifies (Mark 16:16; Acts 22:16).[69] Baptism is a sign of God's promise, giving us comfort that our sins are washed away by the blood of Christ and the Spirit of God, through faith.

God is the primary agent in baptism; baptism is a *means* of grace.[70] Through the minister who baptizes in the Triune name, God gives grace and seals the death, burial, resurrection, and cleansing of Christ upon the heart of the person being baptized. How does baptism assure a believer that Christ's sacrifice benefits him or her personally? The Heidelberg Catechism answers beautifully: "Christ instituted this outward washing and with it promised that, as surely as water washes away the dirt from the body, so certainly his blood and his Spirit wash away my soul's impurity, that is, all my sins."[71]

Likewise, the Lord's Supper, says Bavinck, "is a spiritual meal at which Christ feeds our souls with his crucified body and shed blood. Eating and drinking them serves to strengthen our spiritual, that is, our eternal life, for those who eat the flesh of the Son of Man and drink his blood have eternal life and are raised up on the last day (John 6:54)."[72] Neither the baptismal water nor the bread and wine are magical, but when the church gathers on the Lord's Day and God's people partake of the sacraments by faith, Christ is at work through His Word and Spirit to impart grace to His embattled sheep.[73] Christ is *spiritually* present in the Lord's Supper as the Holy Spirit gives the believer a taste of Heaven (1 Cor 10:16).[74]

The weary pilgrim meets Christ week after week through Word, sacrament, and prayer.[75] Prayer is a means of grace because of Christ's intercession at the Father's right hand.[76] Prayer beseeches our High Priest and Mediator, the very One who is nourishing and protecting us. Prayer is the instrument appointed by God to carry out His will, and, in so doing, our wills are being aligned with His (Job 42:7-9; Matt 6:10; 1 John 5:14).[77] Prayer shows that we are utterly dependent upon God, who welcomes us to bring our requests to Him. Both private and corporate prayers are a means of grace,[78] but there is something special about the church body united in prayer. Hart and Meuther write that "corporate prayer knits the hearts of church members together."[79]

Prayer is also vital to proper thinking and believing. John Bunyan said, "The truths that I know best I have learned on my knees. I never know a thing well till it is burned into my heart by prayer."[80] Pray through the Psalms, the Beatitudes, the Apostles' Creed, or a catechism until those truths are "burned into your heart." Indeed, thinking God's thoughts after Him is an endeavor that is sustained by a diligent prayer life.

Word, sacrament, and prayer—the ordinary means of grace—are vital for a proper context of reading and thinking Scripture. These were the very things that the early church was "devoted to" (i.e., *busied with*; προσκαρτερέω): "So those who received his word were baptized, and there were added that day about three thousand souls. And they devoted themselves to the apostles' teaching and the fellowship, to the breaking of bread and the prayers" (Acts 2:41-42).[81]

Finally, to our last question, let us consider the *ordinariness* of the means of grace. This particular idea goes against some of our modern sensibilities. We tend to look down on the ordinary and favor the radical and revolutionary. We look for the over-the-top, the "next big thing." We live from mountaintop experience to mountaintop experience. We seek out excitement, and, when it cools and wanes, we seek another excitement, a bigger excitement. But all of this leaves us restless and adrift in the sea of sensationalism and consumerism. We judge our spiritual lives by our level of excitement, all the while missing Christ, who is objectively present in Word and sacrament.

Tish Harrison Warren rightly said, "For those of us—and there are a lot of us—who are drawn to an edgy, sizzling spirituality, we need to embrace radical ordinariness and to be grounded in the challenges of the stable mundaneness of the well-lived Christian life."[82] "Spiritual storm-chasing" will only leave us restless.[83] The ordinary means of grace help us to be

grounded and they teach us that, even when we are in a spiritual valley or an emotional dark place, Christ is working on us,
feeding us, and strengthening us each Lord's Day through Word
and sacrament. Even when we don't "feel" it, Christ is objectively there, regardless of our emotional state. The ordinary rhythm
from Lord's Day to Lord's Day is what grounds and gives roots to
our Christian lives.[84] We should not forget that God does *ex-
traordinary* things through the *ordinary* means which He has
instituted.[85]

This realization is vital to a proper context of reading, thinking, and growing in Scripture. The growing Christian ought to
have a rhythm of weekly liturgical worship where he or she receives the ordinary means of grace. Outside of this rhythm of
dependence, the context of reading and thinking Scripture will
be languid and maybe even corrosive.[86]

Element Three: Pastoral Care

A Christian reading Scripture and thinking God's thoughts
after Him will thrive under good pastoral care. It is important to
remember that Christ is the head of the church (Col 1:18). The
pastors are not the head of the church. The deacons are not the
head of the church. The collective members of the church are
not the head of the church. Christ is the Head, and He rules His
church through His Word and Spirit as His faithful pastors over-
see His church and lead His sheep in the exercise of the keys of
His kingdom.[87] At a fundamental level, the church is a monar-
chy ruled by King Jesus, not a democracy.[88]

As the apostles went to be with the Lord, Christ set up two
offices in His church, namely, those of elder and deacon. In Acts
chapter 20, Paul called the elders (πρεσβυτέρος) of the church in
Ephesus to come to him (20:17). He exhorts them: "[P]ay careful

attention to yourselves and to all the flock, in which the Holy Spirit has made you overseers" (20:28). The Holy Spirit not only made them "overseers" (ἐπίσκοπος) but tasked them to *pastor* (*shepherd*, ποιμαίνω) the church (20:28). The titles "elder," "overseer," and "pastor" refer to the same church office.[89]

The "council" of elders that rule or lead the church (sometimes called the "session" or "consistory"; Acts 14:23; 1 Tim 4:14; 5:17)[90] are by no means perfect, but they have been called by the Holy Spirit (Acts 20:28; 1 Pet 5:2-3), they possess good character (1 Tim 3:1-7), and they know the difference between sound doctrine and heterodoxy (Titus 1:5-9). These men have the difficult task of caring for those who are perishing, seeking the lost, healing the broken, and sustaining the healthy (in contrast to the "worthless shepherd" of Zech 11:16). Moreover, they will incur stricter judgment and will have to give an account to God for how they have shepherded His flock (Heb 13:17; James 3:1; cf. Gen 31:38-40).

We should honor the pastors of the church as those sent by Christ to shepherd His flock. On one occasion, Martin Luther spoke harshly against another minister of the gospel. This other minister was a radical and probably deserved rebuke. However, Luther's wife, Katie, rebuked Martin for speaking so coarsely about a minister of the gospel.[91] Like Katie Luther, we should have the proper respect and esteem toward the elders that Christ has given us. No doubt, pastors too live lives of repentance and, sometimes, they even have to be removed from office (1 Tim 5:19-22); but if the Holy Spirit has called these men, let us give them our upmost respect.

The faithful minister, says Gerberding, is a preacher, a shepherd (*seelsorger* in German), and a catechist, who has been objectively called by the Holy Spirit to serve Christ's Church.[92] We live in an anti-authoritarian age, but we should look to our pastors as spiritual doctors who are going to look after our spiritual health until we leave this world to be with our Chief Shepherd, Jesus Christ. We should submit to them (Heb 13:17), insofar as they do not contradict Scripture (Acts 5:29), because they have been tasked by God to exercise oversight of His church (1 Pet 5:1-4).

Our thinking should be done in a context where Christ's ambassadors are watching over our souls, disciplining us when we sin, and seeing to it that we have a healthy diet of sound doctrine. Our pastors instruct us in the ways of Christ, but that is not all they do. Harold Senkbeil rightly said, "Pastors do not teach mere ideas or concepts; by their ministrations they bring Jesus himself into the hearts and lives of people."[93] Christ is pleased to use the tools given to our pastors—namely, Word and sacrament—to bless His children. Is there a better context for thinking God's thoughts after Him than one in which Christ Himself is communing with His Church through Word and sacrament, which are being heralded and administered by Christ's faithful men?

—————▼—————

This chapter has considered the context of a proper reading of and thinking through Scripture. Sound doctrine is not to be learned in a vacuum but in the context of the body of Christ. Children learn well in a context where there is discipline and instruction in the home, as well as faithful church attendance. Christians are born again and given the Holy Spirit and are therefore in the proper *internal* context for right thinking. Christians also participate in the proper *external* context, which has a weekly rhythm of liturgical worship, the ordinary means of grace, and pastoral care and oversight. In Christ's church, says Alford, "God has established a promised delivery system of spiritual blessing for his people."[94] If we are going to grow in the ways that Christ wants us to grow, we cannot neglect the context in which we are called to grow. That is, we must cherish, serve, and submit to the local church, wherein the word is faithfully preached, the sacraments are faithfully administered, and the pastors/elders/overseers faithfully shepherd the flock. The Christian who desires to think God's thoughts after Him does not go to church merely because it is commanded in Scripture (Ex 20:8; Heb 10:25) but because he wants to be fed—nay, he *needs* to be fed!

> Then let us feast this joyful day
> on Christ, the bread of heaven;
> the Word of grace hath purged away
> the old and evil leaven.
> Christ alone our souls will feed,
> he is our meat and drink indeed;
> faith lives upon no other. Hallelujah![95]

PILGRIM THINKING

A s we come to the final chapter of the book, I would like for us to remember who we are. We who have been born again by the Spirit and have come to Christ in faith and repentance also *belong* to Christ. He is our life. We are seated with Him now in the heavenly places (Eph 2:6). This reality should impact how we live here and now:

> If then you have been raised with Christ, seek the things that are above, where Christ is, seated at the right hand of God. Set your minds on things that are above, not on things that are on earth. For you have died, and your life is hidden with Christ in God. When Christ who is your life appears, then you also will appear with him in glory. (Col 3:1-4)

Our citizenship is in Heaven (Phil 3:20), and we are passing through this world to our heavenly home with Christ. We are pilgrims and sojourners. Peter addressed the church as "sojourners and exiles" (1 Pet 2:11). The pilgrim life is nothing new to God's people (1 Chron 29:15). Even the saints in the Old

Testament "acknowledged that they were strangers and exiles on the earth" (Heb. 11:13). They were "seeking a homeland," for they desired a "better country, that is, a heavenly one" prepared for them by God (Heb 11:14-16).

Our pilgrim identity will become very important for the church as persecution and marginalization increase. Living in a post-Christian climate—a climate in which "cultural Christianity" is dead—will force the church to remember who she is. Instead of idolizing bodies, buildings, and budgets,[1] the church must look to Christ in Word and sacrament. When these worldly and fickle metrics dominate our attention and focus, we risk missing Christ who is objectively present in the ordinary means of grace.

The transition from cultural Christianity to a post-Christian culture will not be easy. Church buildings might have to be sold and the programs of yesteryear might have to be cut. But we ought never to forget: the church is the people, not the building or the programs she offers. The church is an assembly of people—a *pilgrim* people who gather to sing praises to God and to fellowship with Christ through Word and sacrament. If we are pilgrims, we must start thinking like pilgrims.

This does not mean that we become apathetic to what is happening around us. We are called to be *involved* pilgrims: we vote, we plead for justice, we give to the poor, we evangelize, we try to make this world better. Yet, we dare not become worldly or entangled in earthly pursuits (2 Tim 2:4).

Geerhardus Vos lamented that our "modern Christian life so often lacks the poise and stability of the eternal." When this happens the church's "purposes turn fickle and unsteady; its methods become superficial and ephemeral; it alters its course so constantly; it borrows so readily from sources beneath itself." To correct this, he says, "we must learn again to carry a heaven-fed and heaven-centered spirit into our walk and work below."[2]

Our pilgrim identity impacts every area of our lives. If we are heading toward the heavenly city of Zion on the narrow path (Prov 4:25-27; Matt 7:13-14), then everything in life is subservient to this pilgrimage. Jonathan Edwards explained:

> *This life ought to be spent by us as to be only a journey or pilgrimage toward heaven....* [The] journey's end is in [the traveler's] mind. If he meets with comfortable accommodations at an inn, he entertains no thoughts of settling there. He considers these things are not his own, that he is but a stranger.... All other concerns of life ought to be entirely subordinate to this.—When a man is on a journey, all the steps he takes are subordinate to the aim of getting to his journey's end.... It was never designed by God that this world should be our home. Neither did God give us these temporal accommodations for that end. If God has given us ample estates, and children or other pleasant friends, it is with no such design, that we should be furnished here, as for a settled abode.... Labour [rather] to have your heart taken up so much about heaven, and heavenly enjoyments, as that you may rejoice when God calls you to leave your best earthly friends and comforts for heaven, there to enjoy God and Christ.... Let it [furthermore] be considered that if our lives be not a journey towards heaven, they will be a journey to hell.[3]

As pilgrims, we have a purpose and a mission. We are going somewhere. We wake up in the morning and our pilgrimage continues. The Bible instructs us on the path that we are to take and it whets our appetite for the world to come.[4] Christ has removed our sin-burden (Ps 38:4) and bids us to flee from the wrath to come (Luke 3:7), for this present world will be destroyed by fire (2 Pet 3:7-13; 1 John 2:15-17). Even in the midst of danger and threat of persecution, we must press on as pilgrims and sojourners.

In John Bunyan's classic, *The Pilgrim's Progress*, Christian (the main character) receives a report of danger ahead. Some were bidding him to turn back and to abandon his pilgrimage to the heavenly city. Christian said, "If I go back to mine own country, that is prepared for fire and brimstone, and I shall certainly perish there; if I can get to the celestial city, I am sure to be in safety there: I must venture. To go back is nothing but death: to go forward is fear of death, and life everlasting beyond it: I will yet go forward."[5] Our pilgrimages pass through dangerous areas (Luke 9:23; Acts 14:22), but we must say with Christian: "I will yet go forward." Christ Himself has given us these marching orders: "Be faithful unto death, and I will give you the crown of life" (Rev 2:10).

The pilgrim motif also shapes how we think in general. Believers have been "lifted into the heavenly world to come," while unbelievers are "bound to the carnal patters of life inherent in this present evil age."[6] The Christian pilgrim takes his cues from the world to come. For the unbeliever, however, this world is all there is—or so he thinks. If we are pilgrims, our minds are instructed by the world to come, shaped by the world to come, and focused on the world to come. And only when the pilgrim's mind is Heaven-saturated can he be of any earthly good to those around him.

———————▼———————

The Bible teaches that we are pilgrims and strangers, walking the narrow path to our heavenly home. This not only changes our lives but also our thinking. If we have been raised with

Christ and are seated with Him in the heavenly places, then our minds, our hearts, and our strength is oriented to our goal of dwelling with Christ. There is an *already, not yet* tension: we are already seated with Christ, but we long for our journey to be complete (Phil 1:23). Furthermore, the Christian pilgrim avoids the earthly, unspiritual, and demonic wisdom that is prevalent in our day (James 3:13-15), seeking, rather, the wisdom from above (James 3:17-18) as he walks by faith, not by sight (2 Cor 5:7).

> Hobgoblin nor foul fiend
> Can daunt his spirit,
> He knows he at the end
> Shall life inherit.
> Then fancies fly away,
> He'll fear not what men say,
> He'll labor night and day
> To be a pilgrim.[7]

APPENDIX

FIFTY-FIVE BOOKS FOR THE GROWING CHRISTIAN

Beginner Level

1. *What is the Gospel?* by Greg Gilbert
2. *The Apostles' Creed: Discovering Authentic Christianity in an Age of Counterfeits* by R. Albert Mohler Jr.
3. *Prayer: Experiencing Awe and Intimacy with God* by Timothy Keller
4. *The 10 Commandments: What They Mean, Why They Matter, and Why We Should Obey Them* by Kevin DeYoung
5. *The Pilgrim's Progress* by John Bunyan
6. *Seeing and Savoring Jesus Christ* by John Piper
7. *The Gospel-Shaped Life* by Ian Hamilton

Basic Level

8. *God Is: A Devotional Guide to the Attributes of God* by Mark Jones
9. *Even Better Than Eden: Nine Ways the Bible's Story Changes Everything about Your Story* by Nancy Guthrie
10. *Jesus on Every Page: 10 Simple Ways to Seek and Find Christ in the Old Testament* by David Murray
11. *A Peculiar Glory: How the Christian Scriptures Reveal Their Complete Truthfulness* by John Piper
12. *Knowing Christ* by Mark Jones

13. *Luther on the Christian Life: Cross and Freedom* by Carl R. Trueman
14. *Fellowship with God* by Martyn Lloyd-Jones
15. *Counseling the Hard Cases: True Stories Illustrating the Sufficiency of God's Resources in Scripture,* ed. by Stuart Scott and Health Lambert
16. *Untangling Emotions* by J. Alasdair Groves and Winston T. Smith
17. *Ordinary: Sustainable Faith in a Radical World* by Michael Horton
18. *Watchfulness: Recovering a Lost Spiritual Discipline* by Brian G. Hedges
19. *Fighting Satan: Knowing His Weakness, Strategies, and Defeat* by Joel R. Beeke
20. *When Sinners Say "I Do": Discovering the Power of the Gospel for Marriage* by Dave Harvey
21. *Doxology: How Worship Works* by Nicolas Alford
22. *Blame It on the Brain? Distinguishing Chemical Imbalances, Brain Disorders, and Disobedience* by Edward T. Welch
23. *21 Servants of Sovereign Joy: Faithful, Flawed, and Fruitful* by John Piper
24. *The Creedal Imperative* by Carl R. Trueman
25. *The Valley of Vision,* a collection of Puritan Prayers
26. *Five Points: Towards A Deeper Experience of God's Grace* by John Piper
27. *The Saint and His Saviour: The Work of the Spirit in the Life of the Christian* by Charles Haddon Spurgeon
28. *Grace Alone: Salvation as Gift of God* by Carl R. Trueman
29. *Concise Theology* by J. I. Packer
30. *Confessions* by St. Augustine
31. *Shepherding a Child's Heart* by Tedd Tripp

Intermediate Level

32. *Redeeming Science: A God-Centered Approach* by Vern S. Poythress
33. *The Majesty of Mystery: Celebrating the Glory of an Incomprehensible God* by K. Scott Oliphint

NOTES

Introduction

[1] Words like "catechist" or "catechism" might be seen as archaic and ancient; some wonder if it is worth retaining these words. Maybe it would be better to update and modernize? I agree with David Rueter: "Yet, I would argue that when we lose terms like *catechesis*, we run the risk of losing the essential core of the Church practice that the term defines." David L. Rueter, *Teaching the Faith at Home: What Does this Mean? How is this Done?* (Concordia, 2016), 7. Rueter explains catechesis: "Thus, the educational process of catechesis is the sounding again of the historic truths of the Christian faith from one generation to the next." Ibid. "Catechesis," of course, means "to give instruction," "to sound again," or even "to echo." Rueter comments, "The Greek word *katacheo*, from which our term *catechesis* is derived means 'to sound again.'" Ibid; Gerberding elaborates even more, writing that "catechesis" is "a compound word. The Greek noun is ἦχος, which means sound, a spoken word, a word sounded back, an echo.... Classically it was used of the sounding down of the rushing water, of the sound of music falling from the ship on the sea. Then it came to signify the sounding down of a word or words of command or instruction from a superior to an inferior, from a teacher to a pupil. The preposition κατά strengthens the meaning, bringing out more emphatically the back or return sound, the echo, the answer. Thus it came to mean instruction by word of mouth, familiar, conversational instruction, a free informal discussion between teacher and pupil." George Henry Gerberding, *The Lutheran Catechist* (The Lutheran Publication Society, 1910), 21-22

[2] Gerberding said, "In all his work the good Catechist constantly endeavors to train and develop the mind, as well as to impart instruction. He desires to promote clear thinking as well as right knowing. He should teach both how to think and what to believe. The two should always go together." Gerberding, *The Lutheran Catechist,* 22-23.

[3] J. Brandon Burks, *Internalizing the Faith: A Pilgrim's Catechism* (Fontes Press, 2018).

[4] For a critique of these secular methods and a commendation of the Christian approach, see Herman Bavinck, *Christian Worldview*, trans. and ed. by Nathaniel Gray Sutanto, James Eglington, and Cory C. Brock (Crossway, 2019), 31-55.

[5] John M. Frame, *A History of Western Philosophy and Theology* (P&R, 2015), 742.

[6] Ibid., 22.

[7] Ibid., 252.

[8] Cornelius Van Til, *Common Grace and the Gospel*, 2nd edition, ed. by K. Scott Oliphint (P&R, 2015), 191.

[9] Oliphint says, "[R]eason's finest hour can only be realized as it is nurtured, caused to grow, and produced within the warmth of Christian faith." K. Scott Oliphint, "Covenant Model," in *Four Views on Christianity and Philosophy* (Zondervan, 2016), 97.

[10] Referred to as the *principium cognoscendi* and *principium essendi*, respectively. See: K. Scott Oliphint, "Because It Is the Word of God," in *Did God Really Say? Affirming the Truthfulness and Trustworthiness of Scripture*, ed. by David B. Garner (P&R, 2012), 1-22; K. Scott Oliphint and Lane G. Tipton, *Revelation and Reason: New Essays in Reformed Apologetics* (P&R, 2007), 279-303.

[11] B. B. Warfield, *The Religious Life of Theological Students* (P&R, 1911), 6.

[12] "Thy Strong Word" (Concordia Publishing House, 1969), accessed 20 January 2020, https://stpaulsfw.org/images/weeks-message/hymn-text/LSB-578-Thy-Strong-Word.pdf.

Chapter 1

[1] Peter A. Lillback and Richard B. Gaffin, Jr., *Thy Word is Still Truth: Essential Writings on the Doctrine of Scripture from the Reformation to Today* (P&R, 2013), 1207-1222.

[2] "Note carefully that this view of inspiration does not imply divine dictation, with human authors limited to the role of secretary. To the contrary, verbal inspiration (specifically, a. verbal plenary understanding of inspiration) affirms that God, through the Holy Spirit, sovereignly superintended the lives of the human authors and made intentional use of their own individuality. Through the work of the Holy Spirit, the human authors of Scripture freely wrote what the Holy Spirit divinely inspired, so that when the Scripture speaks, God speaks... In other words, God wrote a book. He did so through human authors he selected and prepared. By the Holy Spirit, the human authors of Scripture were guided into truth and protected from all error." R. Albert Mohler, "When the Bible Speaks, God Speaks: The Classic Doctrine of Biblical Inerrancy," in *Five Views on Biblical Inerrancy* (Zondervan, 2013), 38, 45.

[3] Vern Sheridan Poythress, *Inerrancy and the Gospels: A God-Centered Approach to the Challenge of Harmonization* (Crossway, 2012), 183. Poythress discusses issues raised in the various Gospel accounts. Why might two Gospel writers report something in different ways and in a different order? There may be several things at work, depending

on the specific account one is speaking about. It could be that there were two different sayings or events that were just similar. Jesus would have preached similar mes-
sages as He went from town to town. Or perhaps one writer simply emphasizes one
particular aspect of the event. Jesus's words may have been long and developed, but a
writer only selected a portion. Augustine taught that God "has the authority to reex-
press himself, to say the same thing in different words." Quoted in Poythress, *Inerrancy and the Gospels*, 191.

[4] E. J. Young, *Thy Word is Truth: Some Thoughts on the Biblical Doctrine of Inspiration*
(William B. Eerdmans, 1957; reprint, Banner of Truth, 2008), 80.

[5] "God is the primary author of Scripture, and men are instrumental secondary authors. And, if instruments, then what men write down is as much God's own words as
if he had written it down without human mediation." K. Scott Oliphint, "Because It Is
the Word of God," in *Did God Really Say? Affirming the Truthfulness and Trustworthiness of Scripture*, ed. by David B. Garner (P&R, 2012), 17.

[6] For a discussion about the canon and why, for example, the New Testament has 27
books, see: Michael J. Kruger, *Canon Revisited: Establishing the Origins and Authority of
the New Testament Books* (Crossway, 2012).

[7] When we say, "The Bible is inerrant," we mean "Our copy of the Bible is inerrant
insofar as it faithfully represents the original autographs." For discussion on this, see:
John Piper, *A Peculiar Glory: How the Christian Scriptures Reveal Their Complete Truthfulness* (Crossway, 2016), 76-86; See also: Richard B. Gaffin, Jr., *God's Word in Servant-
Form: Abraham Kuyper and Herman Bavinck on the Doctrine of Scripture* (Reformed
Academic Press, 2008), 46. Augustine said to Jerome: "I confess to thy love that I have
learned to give this reverence and honor to those books of Scripture alone which are
now called canonical, as firmly to believe that no one of their authors erred in writing
anything... but I so read the others, that however excellent in purity of doctrine, I do
not therefore take a thing to be true because they thought so; but because they persuade me, either through those canonical authors, or probable reason, that it does not
differ from the truth. Nor do I think that you, my brother, are of a different opinion. I
say, further, I do not suppose that you wish your books to be read as if they were the
writings of the prophets or apostles, which beyond a doubt are free from any error." As
quoted in: Francis Turretin, *Institutes of Elenctic Theology*, Vol 1, trans. by George Musgrave Giger, ed. by James T. Dennison, Jr. (P&R, 1992), 164.

[8] "Infallibility means that something *cannot* err, while inerrancy means that it *does not*
err." R. C. Sproul, *What is Reformed Theology? Understanding the Basics* (Baker, 1997),
48.

[9] See: Lillback and Gaffin, *Thy Word is Still Truth*, 560-565.

[10] The Chicago Statement on Biblical Inerrancy, Article XIII. See: Wayne Grudem,
Systematic Theology: An Introduction to Biblical Doctrine (Zondervan, 1994), 1206.

[11] The 1689 Baptist Confession states, "The authority of the Holy Scripture, for which it
ought to be believed, dependeth not upon the testimony of any man or church, but

wholly upon God (who is truth itself), the author thereof; therefore it is to be received because it is the Word of God. We may be moved and induced by the testimony of the church of God to an high and reverent esteem of the Holy Scriptures; and the heavenliness of the matter, the efficacy of the doctrine, and the majesty of the style, the consent of all the parts, the scope of the whole (which is to give all glory to God), the full discovery it makes of the only way of man's salvation, and many other incomparable excellencies, and entire perfections thereof, are arguments whereby it doth abundantly evidence itself to be the Word of God; yet notwithstanding, our full persuasion and assurance of the infallible truth, and divine authority thereof, is from the inward work of the Holy Spirit bearing witness by and with the Word in our hearts" (1.4-5); Turretin also commented, "That the authority of the Scriptures either as to itself or as to us does not depend upon the testimony of the church is proved: (1) because the church is built upon the Scripture (Eph. 2:20) and borrows all authority from it." Turretin, *Institutes*, I:88.

[12] "The highest proof of Scripture derives in general from the fact that God in person speaks in it.... Let this point therefore stand: that those whom the Holy Spirit has inwardly taught truly rest upon Scripture, and that Scripture indeed is self-authenticated; hence, it is not right to subject it to proof and reasoning. And the certainty it deserves with us, it attains by the testimony of the Spirit. For even if it wins reverence for itself by its own majesty, it seriously affects us only when it is sealed upon our hearts through the Spirit. Therefore, illuminated by his power, we believe neither by our own nor by anyone else's judgment that Scripture is from God; but above human judgment we affirm with utter certainty (just as if we were gazing upon the majesty of God himself) that it has flowed to us from the very mouth of God by the ministry of men. We seek no proofs, no marks of genuineness upon which our judgment may lean; but we subject our judgment and wit to it as to a thing far beyond guesswork!" John Calvin, *The Institutes of the Christian Religion*, vol.1, trans. by Ford Lewis Battles, ed. by John T. McNeill (Westminster John Knox, 1960), I.7.4-5. Scott Oliphint helpfully defines what self-attestation *is* and what it *is not*: "We should be clear that self-attestation does not mean self-evident. Self-authentication, or attestation, is an objective attribute, whereas self-evident refers more specifically to the knowing agent. It therefore does not mean that revelation as self-authenticated compels agreement. That which is self-authenticating can be denied. What it means is that it needs no other authority as confirmation in order to be justified and absolutely authoritative in what it says." Oliphint, *Did God Really Say?*, 14. Likewise, Kruger: "We tend to think that we are not justified in holding a belief unless it can be authenticated on the basis of other beliefs. But... this approach overlooks the unique nature of the canon. The canon, as God's Word, is not just true, but the criterion of truth. It is an ultimate authority.... If we try to validate an ultimate authority by appealing to some other authority, then we have just shown that it is not really the ultimate authority." Kruger, *Canon Revisited*, 91-94.

[13] Cornelius Van Til writes that Scripture "comes to the sinner with a claim of absolute authority over man. It asks man to submit his thought captive to it in obedience." Cornelius Van Til, *An Introduction to Systematic Theology: Prolegomena and the Doctrines of Revelation, Scripture, and God*, 2nd ed., ed. by William Edgar (P&R, 2007), 226.

[14] David Garner elaborates, "Perspicuity of divine words necessarily exist because of the Speaker's identity, the eternally coherent God, who has condescended to communicate clearly to those made in his image." David Garner, "Did God Really Say?" in *Did God Really Say? Affirming the Truthfulness and Trustworthiness of Scripture*, ed. by David Garner (P&R, 2012), 151.

[15] Cornelius Van Til, "Nature and Scripture," in *The Infallible Word: A Symposium by the Members of the Faculty of Westminster Theological Seminary* (P&R, 1967), 269; cf. 267.

[16] George Herbert, "The H. Scriptures II," in *A Year With George Herbert: A Guide to Fifty-Two of His Best Loved Poems*, ed. Jim Scott Orrick (Wipf and Stock, 2011), 63.

[17] Ibid.

[18] For a great biography of Martin Luther, see: Carl R. Trueman, *Luther on the Christian Life: Cross and Freedom* (Crossway, 2015), 142-144.

[19] As quoted in: Carl Trueman, *Grace Alone: Salvation as a Gift of God* (Zondervan, 2017), 183.

[20] While affirming this truth of God's provision, we want to stay clear of the prosperity gospel, which teaches that God wants you to be happy, healthy, and prosperous. The Christian life is a call to suffer and yet rejoice at all times. The Christian pilgrimage is very difficult. Jesus said we will take up our cross (execution device) daily. On December 29, 2012 John Piper preached a phenomenal sermon along these lines, entitled, "Sorrowful, Yet Always Rejoicing." I would recommend it: https://www.desiringgod.org/messages/sorrowful-yet-always-rejoicing.

[21] "Lord, Keep Us Steadfast in Your Word," by Martin Luther, trans. Catherine Winkworth, in the Trinity Psalter Hymnal (Committee on Christian Education of the Orthodox Presbyterian Church and the Board of Directors of the United Reformed Churches in North America [USA], 2018), 412.

Chapter 2

[1] Cornelius Van Til, *An Introduction to Systematic Theology*, 2nd edition, ed. by William Edgar (P&R, 2007), 327.

[2] Herman Bavinck, *Reformed Dogmatics: God and Creation*, vol. 2, ed. by John Bolt, trans. by John Vriend (Baker, 2004), 2:152.

[3] "He and he alone is independent. He *is*, in a way no one or nothing else *is*. God alone is the 'I AM.'" K. Scott Oliphint, *Reasons for Faith: Philosophy in the Service of Theology* (P&R, 2006), 174-175.

[4] A. W. Tozer, *The Attributes of God: A Journey into the Father's Heart*, vol. 1 (Christian Publications, 1997), 4.

[5] Mark Jones, *God Is: A Devotional Guide to the Attributes of God* (Crossway, 2017), 64.

[6] Geerhardus Vos, *Reformed Dogmatics*, vol. 1: Theology Proper, trans and ed. by Richard B. Gaffin, Jr. (Lexham, 2014), 1:36.

[7] Bavinck, *Reformed Dogmatics*, 2:196

[8] A. W. Tozer, *The Attributes of God*, 118-120.

[9] Jones, *God Is*, 35, 32.

[10] "God is spirit, infinite, eternal, sovereign, love, just, faithful, patient, gracious, merciful, glorious, holy, unchangeable, without parts, all-knowing, all-wise, all-good, all-present, all-powerful, and of Himself." J. Brandon Burks, *Internalizing the Faith: A Pilgrim's Catechism* (Fontes Press, 2018), 20.

[11] "A created being or a created reality in general cannot furnish a novelty element that is to stand on par with the element of permanency furnished by the Creator. If one believes in the creation doctrine at all, one has to say that the novelty element of the universe is subordinate to the eternal plan of God. Christians believe in two levels of existence, the level of God's existence as self-contained and the level of man's existence as derived from the level of God's existence. For this reason, Christians must also believe in two levels of knowledge, the level of God's knowledge, which is absolutely comprehensive and self-contained, and the level of man's knowledge, which is not comprehensive but is derivative and reinterpretative. Hence we say that as Christians we believe that man's knowledge is analogical of God's knowledge.... [Reformed epistemology] is based upon the Creator-creature distinction. The self-existent God is the original of which man is the derivative.... Whatever is found in man, as God's image-bearer, with the exception of that which results from sin, has its original in God. On the other hand, whatever is found in man's constitution as God's image-bearers exists and acts, when normal, as the derivative of the original in God." Van Til, *An Introduction to Systematic Theology*, 32-33, 72. Herman Bavinck uses classical terminology to get at the Creator-creature distinction: "In reality, God, not the creature, is primary. He is the archetype [the original]; the creature is the ectype [the likeness]. In him everything is original, absolute, and perfect; in creature everything is derived, relative, and limited." Bavinck, *Reformed Dogmatics*, 2:129-130.

[12] The 1689 Baptist Confession of Faith puts it like this: "The distance between God and the creature is so great, that although reasonable creatures do owe obedience to him as their creator, yet they could never have attained the reward of life but by some voluntary condescension on God's part, which he hath been pleased to express by way of covenant" (7.1).

[13] "There is a great chasm fixed between God and his creatures, and the result of such a chasm is that we, all of humanity, could *never* have *any* fruition of God, unless he saw fit voluntarily (graciously), to condescend to us by way of covenant. That condescension includes God's revealing himself in and through his creation, including his word,

to man.... In creating man, God voluntarily determined, at the same time, to establish a relationship with him. That relationship is properly designated a *covenant.*" K. Scott Oliphint, *Covenantal Apologetics: Principles and Practice in Defense of Our Faith* (Crossway, 2013), 43. See also: Samuel Renihan, *The Mystery of Christ: His Covenant and His Kingdom* (Founders Press, 2019), 60.

[14] The Westminster Shorter Catechism Q.12 asks, "What special act of providence did God exercise toward man in the estate wherein he was created" The answer: "When God had created man, he entered into a covenant of life with him, upon condition of perfect obedience; forbidding him to eat of the tree of the knowledge of good and evil, upon the pain of death." Trinity Psalter Hymnal (Committee on Christian Education of the Orthodox Presbyterian Church and the Board of Directors of the United Reformed Churches in North America [USA], 2018), 968.

[15] "Man's interpretations, then, are 'analogical' of God when they reflect, in a finite measure, God's perspective on reality. Capturing the sense of the term 'analogy,' true beliefs are *like* the divine mind as its finite reflections, and *unlike* the divine mind as quantitatively and qualitatively inferior to God's self-contained perspective." B. A. Bosserman, *The Trinity and the Vindication of Christian Paradox: An Interpretation and Refinement of the Theological Apologetic of Cornelius Van Til* (Pickwick, 2014), 112.

[16] As Herman Bavinck explains: "But God is eternal, pure being. And the content of his self-knowledge is no less than this full, eternal, divine being itself. Being and knowing coincide in God. He knows himself through his being. In him consciousness is not the product of a gradual process of development, nor does this consciousness fluctuate from moment to moment, for in him there is no becoming, no process, no development. He is pure being: light without any admixture of darkness.... [H]is knowledge is undivided, simple, unchangeable, eternal. He knows all things instantaneously, simultaneously, from eternity; all things are eternally present to his mind's eye.... God's ideas are absolutely original; they arise from his own being; they are eternal and immutable. Indeed, they are one with his own being. The ideas in God are the very being of God insofar as this being is the pattern of created things and can be expressed and modeled in finite creatures." Bavinck, *Reformed Dogmatics,* 2:195-196, 206. Similarly, Geerhardus Vos wrote that God's knowledge is "that perfection by which, in an entirely unique manner, through His being and with a most simple act, He comprehends Himself and in Himself all that is or could be outside Him." Vos, *Reformed Dogmatics,* 1:16.

[17] "God and his creation differ radically; God's knowledge is original, whereas man's knowledge is derivative; man's knowledge is not identical with but analogous to God's knowledge; man must creaturely and receptively constructively think God's thoughts after him." Hendrick G. Stoker, "Reconnoitering the Theory of Knowledge of Prof. Dr. Cornelius Van Til," in *Jerusalem and Athens: Critical Discussions on the Philosophy and Apologetics of Cornelius Van Til,* ed. by E.R. Geehan (P&R, 1980), 66.

[18] Ibid., 30.

[19] K. Scott Oliphint, *The Majesty of Mystery: Celebrating the Glory of an Incomprehensible God* (Lexham Press, 2016), 46-47.

[20] Bavinck goes on to say that "Scripture is equally far removed from the idea that believers can grasp the revealed mysteries in a scientific sense. In truth, the knowledge that God has revealed of himself in nature and Scripture far surpasses human imagination and understanding. In that sense it is all mystery with which the science of dogmatics is concerned, for it does not deal with finite creatures, but from the beginning to the end looks past all creatures and focuses on the eternal and infinite One himself." Bavinck, *Reformed Dogmatics,* 2:29.

[21] "Christian worship, as well as Christian theology, *begins* with mystery. Mystery is not something that functions simply as a *conclusion* to our thinking about God. It is not that we learn and think and reason as much as we can and then admit in the end that there is some mystery left over. Instead, we *begin* by acknowledging the mystery of God and His ways. We *begin* with the happy recognition that God and His activities are ultimately incomprehensible to us. When we begin with that recognition, we can begin to understand God properly and so worship Him in light of who He is and what He has done." Oliphint, *The Majesty of Mystery,* 5.

[22] Ibid., 8-10.

[23] Bavinck, *Reformed Dogmatics,* vol. 1, 29.

[24] Renihan, *The Mystery of Christ,* 22.

[25] Harold Senkbeil said, "Mystery remains forever inaccessible to human scrutiny. Yet mystery revealed provides access to the inaccessible." Harold L. Senkbeil, *The Care of Souls: Cultivating a Pastor's Heart* (Lexham, 2019), 11.

[26] "Immortal, Invisible, God Only Wise," by Walter C. Smith, in the Trinity Hymnal: Baptist Edition (Great Commission Publications, 1995), 35.

Chapter 3

[1] John Calvin, *The Institutes of the Christian Religion*, ed. by John T. McNeill, trans. by Ford Lewis Battles (Westminster John Knox Press, 1960), I.1.1.

[2] "The system that Christians seek to obtain may, by contrast, be said to be *analogical. By this is meant that God is the original and that man is the derivative. God has absolute self-contained system within himself.* What comes to pass in history happens in accord with that system or plan by which he orders the universe. *But man, as God's creature, cannot have a replica of that system of God. He cannot have a reproduction of that system.* He must, to be sure, think God's thoughts after him; but this means that he must, in seeking to form his own system, constantly be subject to the authority of God's system *to the extent* that this is revealed to him." Cornelius Van Til, *A Christian Theory of Knowledge* (P&R, 1969), 16 (emphasis original).

3 Jim Scott Orrick, *A Year with George Herbert: A Guide to Fifty-Two of His Best Loved Poems* (Wipf and Stock, 2011), 61; cf. 61 n.13, 14.

4 Martin Luther, *Galatians*, ed. by Alister McGrath and J. I. Packer (Crossway, 1998), xvii, xx.

5 Cornelius Van Til often depicted the fall in this way. See Cornelius Van Til, "History and Nature of Apologetics: Patterns of Thinking and the Gospel – Part 2" (lecture, Westminster Theological Seminary, Glenside, PA, 1980), http://media1.wts.edu/media/audio/vt202_copyright.mp3.

6 Theologians refer to one's foundation as *principia*. A *principia* is "a beginning point, a source, or a first principle." Therefore, a *principium cognoscendi* is "the principle, source, or foundation of knowing." K. Scott Oliphint, "Because it is the Word of God," in *Did God Really Say? Affirming the Truthfulness and Trustworthiness of Scripture*, ed. by David Garner (P&R, 2012), 2, 5.

7 Cornelius Van Til, *The Defense of the Faith*, 4th edition, ed. by K. Scott Oliphint (P&R, 2008), 57-58, 140.

8 "A persistent reluctance to submit to the plain teaching of the Scripture is a sure indication that you have not repented of your sinful resolve to determine for yourself what is good and evil. You still have the forbidden fruit in your mouth. Spit it out and receive the words of Jesus: 'Whoever hears my word and believes him who sent me has eternal life' (John 5:24)." Jim Scott Orrick, *Mere Calvinism* (P&R, 2019), 16.

9 "The tree is called the tree of 'knowledge of good and evil', because it is the God-appointed instrument to lead man through probation to the state of religious and moral maturity wherewith his highest blessedness is connected.... To attain to a knowledge of good and evil is not necessarily an undesirable and culpable thing. It could happen in a good way, in case man stood in probation, no less than in an evil way, in case man fell. The name is neutral as to its import.... Man was to attain something he had not attained before. He was to learn the good in its clear opposition to the evil, and the evil in its clear opposition to the good.... Had he [Adam] fallen, then the contrast of evil with good would have even more vividly impressed itself upon him, because the remembered experience of choosing the evil and the continuous experience of doing the evil, in contrast with the memory of the good, would have shown most sharply how different the two are. The perception of difference in which the maturity consisted related to the one pivotal point, whether man would make his choice for the sake of God and of God alone." Geerhardus Vos, *Biblical Theology: Old and New Testament* (The Banner of Truth Trust, 2012), 31-32.

10 Brandon Crowe notes that Jesus was tempted as the second Adam and succeeded where the first Adam failed. In the Gospel of Luke, "the temptation is connected to the baptism by means of the genealogy that terminates with Adam, the son of God (Luke 3:38). Thus, not only do we find in Luke the Deuteronomic context of Israel as son of God in the temptation narrative, but the Adamic emphasis of the genealogy leads directly to the testing of Jesus as God's Son. Jesus overcomes temptation in the

postlapsarian wilderness, in contrast to Adam who failed in the garden." Brandon D.
Crowe, *The Last Adam: A Theology of the Obedient Life of Jesus in the Gospels* (Baker
Academic, 2017), 76.

[11] "Exiled from Eden and its holy cosmic mountain, they would construct from the
cursed ground upward their own staircase-mountain to the gods. Such were the ziggu-
rats.... The Lord was going to restore the paradise order with its mountain of God (cf.
Sinai and Zion, type and antitype) as a gift of redemptive grace, but they attempted to
gain immortality by their own work." Meredith G. Kline, *Genesis: A New Commentary*,
ed. by Jonathan G. Kline (Hendrickson, 2016), 48.

[12] Van Til explains, "When on the created level of existence man thinks God's thoughts
after him, that is, when man thinks in self-conscious submission to the voluntary
revelation of the self-sufficient God, he has therewith the only possible ground of
certainty for his knowledge." Cornelius Van Til, "Nature and Scripture," in *The Infallible
Word: A Symposium by the Members of the Faculty of Westminster Theological Seminary*, 2nd ed, ed. N. B. Stonehouse and Paul Woolley (P&R, 1967), 278. Nevertheless,
"thinking God's thoughts after Him" is not to forsake one's reason or experience; rather, it refers to bringing one's faculties under the authority of God. As Greg Bahnsen
has stated, "When man knows things revealed in Scripture or in the natural world, he
is thinking God's thoughts after Him.... Thinking God's thoughts after Him requires
that men think logically and conceptually, as well as learn things through observation
(using their senses). The Christian worldview provides a context within which rational
and empirical knowing are intelligible." Greg L. Bahnsen, *Van Til's Apologetic: Readings and Analysis* (P&R, 1998), 244. Van Til states further, "The sinner seeks a criterion
of truth and knowledge independent of the revelation of God. The sinner wants to test
that which presents itself as the revelation of God by a standard not itself taken from
his revelation." Cornelius Van Til, *A Christian Theory of Knowledge*, 33.

[13] Bahnsen, *Van Til's Apologetic*, 1, n.2.

[14] "In order for someone to understand one fact properly, that fact needs to be seen in
the context of God's plan and purposes." K. Scott Oliphint, *Covenantal Apologetics:
Principles and Practice in Defense of Our Faith* (Crossway, 2013), 54.

[15] K. Scott Oliphint, "Covenantal Model," in *Four Views on Christianity and Philosophy*,
ed. by Paul M. Gould and Richard Brian Davis (Zondervan, 2016), 83, cf. 97.

[16] Van Til wrote, "Thus it is impossible for the mind of man to function except in an
atmosphere of revelation. And every thought of man when it functioned normally in
this atmosphere of revelation would express the truth as laid in the creation by God.
Bahnsen, *Van Til's Apologetic*, 167.

[17] Logic and facts, therefore, "have meaning only in terms of the 'story,'" which is to say
that "one must operate within the 'story' of Scripture (the Christian story) in order to
have a true epistemology." William D. Dennison, "Van Til's Epistemology and Analytic
Philosophy," in *In Defense of the Eschaton: Essays in Reformed Apologetics*, ed. by James
Douglas Baird (Wipf & Stock, 2015), 18, 30, 32-33.

[18] Cornelius Van Til, *Christian Theistic Evidences*, 2nd ed., ed. by K. Scott Oliphint (1978; P&R, 2016), 67. Emphasis original.

[19] Even Hume, says Bahnsen, saw that the mind is incapable of organizing power, for "even if all the facts were brought into the mind in the forms of concepts, they would still be utterly unrelated. It would be as though the human mind, like a modern Noah's ark, had gathered together all facts which the womb of chance has produced in the past and would produce in the future, only to realize that the concept of the ark is itself nothing but the faint replica of a percept. Thus all the facts would still be not partially but wholly unknowable.... If there is a segment of reality that he is not aware of and cannot account for or understand (and who could know how extensive it is?), then he cannot be sure that there are not factors that are relevant to, or would interfere with, the adequacy of the explanations he has offered for what he experiences. If his explanatory principles cannot be thought of as universal, but are subject to possible qualification, he cannot say in any particular case that it is appropriate to use those principles or that he is not being arbitrary or shortsighted." Greg L. Bahnsen, *Van Til's Apologetic*, 335, 331 n.146; cf. 304-305, 382-383.

[20] "No other species on this planet has the ability to reason as we do. Not only are we able to reason, we're able to recognize and reflect on our *ability* to reason. We can reason about *reason itself*.... How then do we account for this truly remarkable human ability, this indispensable feature of our lives? Once again we find that the Christian worldview makes excellent sense of this obvious fact. The ultimate reality is a *rational* reality. God is the supreme intellect. Since God is both perfect and personal, He knows and understands all truths; more than that, God knows and understands *how every truth relates to every other truth*. What this means is that our universe has its source in a rational mind. While there are aspects of it that defy *our* rational understanding, the universe as such isn't intrinsically irrational or unintelligible." James N. Anderson, *Why Should I Believe Christianity?*, ed. by James N. Anderson and Greg Welty (Christian Focus, 2016), 116.

[21] "God, Be Merciful to Me," in the Trinity Psalter Hymnal (Committee on Christian Education of the Orthodox Presbyterian Church and the Board of Directors of the United Reformed Churches in North America [USA], 2018), 51C.

Chapter 4

[1] The Westminster Larger Catechism Q.18 says, "God's Works of providence are his most holy, wise, and powerful, preserving and governing all his creatures; ordering them, and all their actions, to his own glory." The Westminster Larger Catechism, in the Trinity Psalter Hymnal (Committee on Christian Education of the Orthodox Presbyterian Church and the Board of Directors of the United Reformed Churches in North America [USA], 2018), 941.

[2] Vern Poythress, *Redeeming Science: A God-Centered Approach* (Crossway, 2006), 177.

[3] Tenth Presbyterian Church in Philadelphia, PA holds an annual Boice Center Inaugural Lecture Series. In 2013 they held a series of lectures on the inerrancy of Scripture. One of those lectures was delivered by Vern Poythress on "Inerrancy and Science," where he discussed the similarities between the attributes of God and the attributes of the scientific laws. You can view the lecture online: https://faculty.wts.edu/lectures/inerrancy-science/.

[4] See: Herman Bavinck, *Philosophy of Revelation*, A New Annotated Edition, eds., Cory Brock and Nathaniel Gray Sutanto (Hendrickson, 2018).

[5] The Belgic Confession, Article 2. See: Liturgical Forms and Prayers of the United Reformed Churches in Northern America Together with the Doctrinal Standards of the URCNA (The United Reformed Churches in North America [Canada], 2018), 139-141.

[6] Special revelation often refers to both Christ and Scripture. "God has now supplemented general revelation with the further revelation of himself as Savior of sinners through Jesus Christ. This revelation, given in history and embodied in Scripture, and opening the door of salvation to the lost, is usually called special or specific revelation." J. I. Packer, *Concise Theology: A Guide to Historic Christian Beliefs* (Tyndale House, 1993), 10.

[7] Poythress, *Redeeming Science,* 33.

[8] "Scientific theories are not the same thing as general revelation. General revelation (like special revelation) refers to an infallible action of God (or to the content revealed through that action). Scientific theories are the fallible interpretation of what Christians know to be God's created works." Keith A. Mathison, *A Reformed Approach to Science and Scripture* (Ligonier Ministries, 2013), chap. 3, Kindle.

[9] "So when we find discrepancies between the Bible and science, we look for where we went astray. Somewhere someone has misinterpreted—whether misinterpreting Scripture, or misinterpreting the world of scientific study, or both!" Poythress, *Redeeming Science,* 43.

[10] "Scripture has a *linguistic* and *redemptive* priority. It has a *linguistic* priority, because it comes to us in human language. By contrast, we do not have access to God's words of providence in *human language*... In this way, the Bible has a kind of *linguistic* ultimacy, in that it is the word of God, not merely a human approximation to the word, a guess at the word on the basis of an accumulation of observations about its effects. My linguistic formulation of the laws of aerodynamics is fallible; the Bible, as *linguistic* communication, is not fallible. In this respect, the formulations by a human scientist are more like a commentary on the Bible than they are like the Bible itself. The commentary, as a human product, is fallible, whereas the Bible is infallible." Ibid., 45.

[11] Ibid., 269-270.

[12] Cornelius Van Til, "Nature and Scripture," in *The Infallible Word: A Symposium by the Members of the Faculty of Westminster Theological Seminary,* 2nd ed., ed. by N. B. Stonehouse and Paul Woolley (P&R, 1967), 267; cf. 269, 273, 275.

13 Poythress, *Redeeming Science*, 158-160, 339

14 "How Great Thou Art," by Carl Gustav Boberg, trans. by Stuart K. Hine, in the Trinity Psalter Hymnal, 227.

Chapter 5

1 "While both the believer and unbeliever are made in the image of God, the unbeliever unrighteously suppresses the truth of God that is revealed to him through creation and makes himself the ultimate judge of truth; whereas the believer submits to God's Word as the ultimate foundation for knowledge and seeks to think God's thoughts after Him." J. Brandon Burks, *Internalizing the Faith: A Pilgrim's Catechism* (Fontes Press, 2018), 49.

2 See: John Murray, "The Imputation of Adam's Sin," in *Justified in Christ: God's Plan for us in Justification*, ed. by K. Scott Oliphint (Mentor, 2007), 205-294. Also see: this question and answer from John Cotton's catechism: "Q. What is your birth-sin? A. Adam's Sin imputed to me, and a corrupt nature dwelling in me," John Cotton, *Milk for Babes. Drawn Out of the Breasts of both Testaments,* reprint (Quinta Press, 2011).

3 See: Richard B. Gaffin Jr., *By Faith, Not by Sight: Paul and the Order of Salvation*, 2nd edition (P&R, 2013).

4 Geerhardus Vos, "The Range of the Logos Title in the Prologue to the Fourth Gospel," in *Redemptive History and Biblical Interpretation: The Shorter Writings of Geerhardus Vos*, ed. Richard B. Gaffin Jr. (P&R, 1980), 50; cf. 76-82; K. Scott Oliphint, *Thomas Aquinas* (P&R, 2017), 31-49.

5 Greg L. Bahnsen, *Van Til's Apologetic: Readings and Analysis* (P&R, 1998), 448.

6 "But he cannot ever completely suppress the knowledge of God and of morality within himself.... God's revelation is everywhere, and everywhere perspicuous." Cornelius Van Til, *Common Grace and the Gospel,* 2nd ed., ed. by K. Scott Oliphint (P&R, 2015), 208-209.

7 Ibid.

8 Cornelius Van Til, *The Defense of the Faith*, 4th ed., ed. by K. Scott Oliphint (P&R, 2008), 196, 258.

9 Bahnsen, *Van Til's Apologetic,* 451.

10 See: John M. Frame, *A History of Western Philosophy and Theology* (P&R, 2015), 481, 743.

11 Christians sometimes disagree on the length of each "day" in Genesis 1. For a comparison of views, see: David G. Hagopian, ed., *The Genesis Debate: Three Views on the Days of Creation* (Crux Press, 2001).

12 K. Scott Oliphint, *Covenantal Apologetics: Principles and Practice in Defense of Our Faith* (Crossway, 2013), 54. Or, as Stoker said, "To be a fact at all it must be a revelational fact. Without the presupposition of God, the whole creation and every fact is meaningless and its interpretation and explanation futile." Hendrick G. Stoker,

"Reconnoitering the Theory of Knowledge of Prof. Dr. Cornelius Van Til," in *Jerusalem and Athens: Critical Discussions on the Philosophy and Apologetics of Cornelius Van Til*, ed. by E.R. Geehan (P&R, 1980), 59.

[13] Richard Baxter, *The Reformed Pastor* (1656; The Banner of Truth, 2012), 56-57.

[14] Richard B. Gaffin Jr., "Epistemological Reflections on 1 Corinthians 2:6-16," in *Revelation and Reason: New Essays in Reformed Apologetics*, ed. by K. Scott Oliphint and Lane G. Tipton (P&R, 2007), 16.

[15] Gaffin shows that in Luke 10:21-22 the inability to receive the revelation is not moral but intellectual. He says, "The categories in view are cognitive... Jesus speaks of the need for *faith*. Just as revelation is necessary, because what is revealed is not an intellectual attainment or any other human accomplishment, so the necessary condition in its recipients is faith, the humility that stems from faith alone; the necessity of revelation involves the necessity of faith." Gaffin, "Epistemological Reflections on 1 Corinthians 2:6-16," 16. Also, as Garner shows, the illumination of the Spirit has to do with the moral side of fallen man. "Illumination coordinates with perspicuity because the Spirit of Truth illumines us to the resident and vital meaning of Scripture. We understand Scripture not because the Holy Spirit takes that which is opaque or translucent and makes it transparent; instead, we understand Scripture because the Holy Spirit transforms us, removing the moral blinders from our hearts' eyes and enabling us to see Scripture for what it is (cf. 2 Tim. 3:16-17; 2 Peter 1:19-21). Perspicuity provides the objective basis for illumination; illumination is not the basis for perspicuity.... Illumination does not change Scripture, it changes us." David Garner, "Did God Really Say?" in *Did God Really Say? Affirming the Truthfulness and Trustworthiness of Scripture*, ed. by David Garner (P&R, 2012), 152.

[16] "The kingdom of God is totalitarian in the most ultimate sense we can know and experience. It is not a partial or part-time allegiance, involving only some of our efforts or just one sector of our experience, or merely a part of our knowledge." Gaffin, "Epistemological Reflections on 1 Corinthians 2:6-16," 18.

[17] Gaffin writes, "[A]ccording to Jesus, revelation is the exclusive and comprehensive *principium* for human knowledge, its foundation and norm. In terms of classical Reformation predicates, revelation involves both a *sola* and a *tota*." Gaffin, "Epistemological Reflections on 1 Corinthians 2:6-16," 19.

[18] This is known as the *transcendental argument* for God's existence. See: Greg Bahnsen and Gordon Stein, "A Transcendental Argument for God's Existence," in *Christian Apologetics: An Anthology of Primary Sources*, ed. by Khaldoun A. Sweis and Chad V. Meister (Zondervan, 2012), 139-167.

[19] See: Geerhardus Vos, "The Eschatological Aspect of the Pauline Conception of the Spirit," in *Redemptive History and Biblical Interpretation: Shorter Writings of Geerhardus Vos*, ed. by Richard B. Gaffin Jr. (P&R, 1980), 91-125.

[20] For a more detailed exposition of 1 Corinthians 2:6-16, see: Richard B. Gaffin Jr., "Epistemological Reflections on 1 Corinthians 2:6-16."

[21] Ibid., 142.

[22] Oliphint, *Covenantal Apologetics*, 52-53.

[23] Ibid.

[24] "But how shall men ever be challenged to look inside themselves and find that all that is not of faith is sin if they are encouraged to think that without the light of Scripture and without the regenerating power of the Holy Spirit they can, at least in the natural sphere, do what is right?... If he is asked to use his reason as the judge of the credibility of the Christian revelation without at the same time being asked to renounce his view of himself as ultimate, then he is virtually asked to believe and to disbelieve in his own ultimacy at the same time and in the same sense." Van Til, *The Defense of the Faith*, 82, 107. Also see: Thom Notaro, *Van Til and the Use of Evidence* (P&R, 1980).

[25] This does not mean that the unbeliever does not know true things. Rather, it means that if the unbeliever's worldview were correct, he or she would not have a basis for knowledge. The fact that unbelievers know things is evidence for the God of Scripture. See: Greg L. Bahnsen, *Presuppositional Apologetics: Stated and Defended*, ed. by Joel McDurmon (American Vision Press and Covenant Media Press, 2008).

[26] Cornelius Van Til, *Christian Apologetics*, 2nd ed., ed. by William Edgar (P&R, 2003), 119.

[27] See: Greg Foster, *The Joy of Calvinism: Knowing God's Personal, Unconditional, Irresistible, Unbreakable Love* (Crossway, 2012).

[28] "Soldiers of Christ, in Truth Arrayed," by Basil Manly, Jr., in The Baptist Hymnal (Convention Press, 1991), 574.

Chapter 6

[1] Oliphint writes, "There is a great chasm fixed between God and his creatures, and the result of such a chasm is that we, all of humanity, could *never* have *any* fruition of God, unless he saw fit, voluntarily (graciously), to condescend to us by way of covenant. That condescension includes God's revealing himself in and through his creation, including his word, to man. We begin, therefore, with respect to who we *are* and to what we can *know*, with a fundamental distinction between the Creator and the creature... Contrary to some opinions, God is in fact Totally Other. But there is nothing intrinsic to this truth that would preclude God from revealing himself to his creatures. Since God is Totally Other from creation, our understanding of him and our communication and communion with him can take place only by his initiative. That initiative is his condescension, including his revelation. Such revelation, as the exclusive means of knowledge of and communion with God, *assumes* rather than *negates* God's utter 'otherness.'" K. Scott Oliphint, *Covenantal Apologetics: Principles and Practice in Defense of Our Faith* (Crossway, 2013), 40-41.

[2] The Westminster Confession of Faith, in the Trinity Psalter Hymnal (Committee on Christian Education of the Orthodox Presbyterian Church and the Board of Directors of the United Reformed Churches in North America [USA], 2018), 923.

[3] J. Brandon Burks, *Internalizing the Faith: A Pilgrim's Catechism* (Fontes Press, 2018), 44.

[4] Ibid.

[5] See: Lane G. Tipton, "The History of Heaven: The Absolute Beginning and Sabbath Rest Before the Law — Genesis 1:1–2:2," 2019 Reformed Forum Theology Conference, accessed October 18, 2019, https://reformedforum.org/podcasts/rf19_02_tipton/.

[6] Ibid. See also: Meredith G. Kline, *God, Heaven and Har Magedon: A Covenantal Tale of Cosmos and Telos* (Wipf and Stock, 2006), 12.

[7] Kline, *God, Heaven and Har Magedon*, 223-250.

[8] Ibid., 13-17.

[9] Vos explains 1 Corinthians 15:44b, "The Apostle was intent on showing that in the plan of God from the outset provision was made for a higher kind of body.... From the abnormal body of sin, no inference could be drawn as to that effect. The abnormal and the eschatological are not so logically correlated that the one can be postulated from the other. But the world of creation and the world to come *are* thus correlated, the one pointing forward to the other; on the principle of typology the first Adam prefigures the last Adam, the psychical body the pneumatic body (cp. Rom. V. 14). The statement of vs 44b is not meant as an apodictic assertion, but as an argument: if there *exists* one kind of body, there *exists* the other kind also." Geerhardus Vos, *The Pauline Eschatology* (1930; P&R, 1994), 169, n. 19.

[10] "In the endoxate Spirit-heaven the revelation of God's Glory was present in substantive form from the beginning. And the prospect of a consummated Epiphanation of the Glory-Spirit, an eternal temple, a heaven peopled with glorified humanity, was proffered from the outset in the promise sanctions of the creation covenant. A primal eschatological paradigm was thereby established in that covenant and basic to it was the goal of a sabbatical consummation of Glory." Kline, *God, Heaven and Har Magedon*, 14; cf. 3-30.

[11] See: Westminster Shorter Catechism Q.1.

[12] This view is opposed to the Roman Catholic doctrine of the donum superadditum. See: Lane G. Tipton, "The Trinity, Creation, and Covenantal Condescension: The Deeper Protestant Conception." 2018 Reformed Forum Theology Conference, accessed July 15, 2019, https://reformedforum.org/podcasts/rf18_02_tipton/.

[13] It is important to note that Adam was oriented toward a place even greater than Eden. Consequently, our hope is not to return to the Garden of Eden. Our hope is a place better than Eden. See: Nancy Guthrie, *Even Better Than Eden* (Crossway, 2018).

[14] Nehemiah Coxe and John Owen, *Covenant Theology: From Adam to Christ*, ed. by Ronald D. Miller, James M. Renihan, and Francisco Orozco (RBAP, 2005), 45, 47.

[15] See: John Murray, "The Imputation of Adam's Sin," in *Justified in Christ: God's Plan for us in Justification*, ed. by K. Scott Oliphint (Mentor, 2007), 205-294.

[16] See: 1689 Baptist Confession 6.1-3; 7.3; Baptist Catechism Q.15-23.

[17] "According to the Master Architect's design for creation, there is yet another phase to be reached in the on-going seventh day of God, another stage in the history of heaven and earth. The King of heaven will at the hour appointed consummate his cosmic temple." Kline, *God, Heaven, and Har Magedon*, 12. The word "consummation" is sometimes found in translations of Daniel 9:27 (כָּלָה), referring to the destruction God has decreed. The word, more broadly, refers to the "end of history and the fulfillment of God's kingdom promises." "Consummation," in *Holman Illustrated Bible Dictionary*, ed. by Chad Brand, Charles Draper, and Archie England (Holman Reference, 2003), 335.

[18] The use of "natural vs. spiritual" language is not intended to set up a Platonic dualism between the physical and the immaterial. In 1 Cor 15, Paul contrasts Adam's pre-fall body with Jesus's post-resurrection body. He calls Adam's pre-fall body a "natural body" and Jesus's post-resurrection body a "spiritual body." In this sense, "spiritual" is very much *physical*. You might say Paul is contrasting a natural-physical body with a spiritual-physical body. Paul says that imbedded into creation itself is a movement from the natural to the spiritual (1 Cor 15:44). Adam failed to bring humanity through this movement, but the second Adam succeeded through His own obedience and blood.

[19] Up to this point, the Reformed Baptists and the Reformed and Presbyterians have been in large agreement. However, there is disagreement on the relationship between the Old and New Covenants. For the Reformed Baptist view, see: Samuel D. Renihan, *From Shadow to Substance: The Federal Theology of the English Particular Baptists (1642-1704)*, Centre for Baptist History and Heritage Studies, vol. 16 (Regent's Park College, 2018); Richard Barcellos, ed., *Recovering a Covenantal Heritage: Essays in Baptist Covenant Theology* (RBAP, 2014); Samuel Renihan, *The Mystery of Christ: His Covenant and His Kingdom* (Founders, 2019). For the Reformed and Presbyterian view, see: Michael Horton, *God of Promise: Introducing Covenant Theology* (Baker, 2006); Meredith G. Kline, *By Oath Consigned: A Reinterpretation of The Covenant Signs Of Circumcision And Baptism* (Eerdmans, 1975); Herman Witsius, *The Economy of Covenants Between God and Man*, vols. 1-2 (Reformation Heritage, 2012).

[20] Jeffery D. Johnson says, "The covenant of grace *is* the covenant of works kept for the elect by Jesus Christ." Jeffery D. Johnson, *The Kingdom of God: A Baptist Expression of Covenant and Biblical Theology* (Free Grace Press, 2014), 144; See also: G. K. Beale, *A New Testament Biblical Theology: The Unfolding of the Old Testament in the New* (Baker Academic, 2011), 298-316.

[21] See: Geerhardus Vos, "The Eschatological Aspect of the Pauline Conception of the Spirit," in *Redemptive History and Biblical Interpretation: Shorter Writings of Geerhardus Vos*, ed. by Richard B. Gaffin, Jr. (P&R, 1980); Geerhardus Vos, "Heavenly-Mindedness," in *Grace and Glory: Sermons Preached in the Chapel of Princeton Theological Seminary* (Solid Ground Christian Books, 2007).

[22] Meredith G. Kline, "The Intrusion and the Decalogue," in *The Structure of Biblical Authority*, 2nd ed. (Wipf and Stock, 1989), 154-171.

[23] Beale, *A New Testament Biblical Theology*, 162. See: Oscar Cullman, *Christ and Time: The Primitive Christian Conception of Time and History*, trans. Floyd V. Filson (Westminster, 1950), 87; Anthony A. Hoekema, *The Bible and the Future* (Eerdmans, 1979), 20-21.

[24] Kline, *God, Heaven and Har Magedon*, 20. Also see: Samuel Renihan, *The Mystery of Christ: His Covenant and His Kingdom* (Founders, 2019), 68.

[25] Van Til speaks about those unbelievers who suppress the truth of God in unrighteousness, saying, "It is rather that in Adam, they had heard this God speak to them and in Adam they had virtually denied his existence. They had with all men in Adam, their representative, denied that space-time reality is dependent upon God, created and controlled by him. They had with all men in Adam assumed not that possibility is subject to God but that God is subject to abstract possibility. When Adam, for all men, refused to take God's prediction of punishment for disobedience seriously, he virtually said that the facts and laws of the universe are not under God's control but operate by virtue of chance." Cornelius Van Til, *The Defense of the Faith*, 4th ed., ed. by K. Scott Oliphint (P&R, 2008), 238.

[26] Van Til wrote, "Weighing and measuring and formal reasoning are but aspects of one unified act of interpretation. It is either the would-be autonomous man, who weighs and measures what he thinks are brute or bare facts by the help of what he thinks of as abstract impersonal principles, or it is the believer, knowing himself to be a creature of God, who weighs and measures what he thinks of as God-created facts by what he thinks of as God-created laws." Cornelius Van Til, *Common Grace and the Gospel*, 2nd ed., ed by K. Scott Oliphint (P&R, 2015), 56.

[27] Lane G. Tipton, "The Holy Spirit, Adam, and the Eschatology of the Covenant of Works" (lecture, Westminster Theological Seminary, Spring 2017).

[28] "It Is Well with My Soul," by Horatio Gates Spafford, in the Trinity Psalter Hymnal, 476.

Chapter 7

[1] "The standard view in theology is that its *principium essendi* is God himself. He alone provides what is needed for us to understand him and his revelation to us. The *principium cognoscendi* is revelation itself. In the Christian sense, the *principium cognoscendi externum* (external principle of knowledge) is God's special revelation in his Word, and the *principium cognoscendi internum* (internal principle of knowledge) is regenerate reason and the Holy Spirit." K. Scott Oliphint, *Reasons for Faith: Philosophy in the Service of Theology* (P&R, 2006), 26.

[2] K. Scott Oliphint, *The Majesty of Mystery: Celebrating the Glory of an Incomprehensible God* (Lexham Press, 2016), 44.

3 B. B. Warfield said, "The older writers discovered intimations of the Trinity in such phenomena as the plural form of the Divine name *Elōhīm*, the occasional employment with reference to God of plural pronouns ('Let us make man in our image,' Gen. i.26; iii.22; xi.7; Isa. vi.8), or plural verbs (Gen. xx.13; xxxv.7), certain repetitions of the name of God which seem to distinguish between God and God (Ps. xlv.6, 7; cx. 1; Hos. i.7), threefold liturgical formulas (Num. vi.24, 26; Isa. vi.3), a certain tendency to hypostatize the conception of Wisdom (Prov. viii), and especially the remarkable phenomena connected with the appearances of the Angel of Jehovah (Gen. xvi.2-13, xxii.11, 16; xxxi.11, 13; xlviii.15-16; Ex. iii.2, 4, 5; Jgs. xiii.20-22)." B. B. Warfield, "Biblical Doctrine of the Trinity," in *Biblical Doctrines* (The Banner of Truth Trust, 1988; reprint, 2002), 140.

4 Ibid., 141-142.

5 For the various terms used to describe the Trinity, see: Richard A. Muller, *Post-Reformation Reformed Dogmatics: The Rise and Development of Reformed Orthodoxy, ca. 1520 to ca. 1725*, vol. 4: The Triunity of God (Baker Academic, 2003), 167-189.

6 The essence of the Son and Spirit are unbegotten. The Son is God of Himself (*autotheos*), as is the Spirit. The Son and Spirit receive their Personhood from the Father, but not their essential deity. See: John Calvin, *The Institutes of the Christian Religion*, ed. by John T. McNeill; trans. by Ford Lewis Battles (Westminster John Knox Press, 1960), I.13.25; Geerhardus Vos, *Reformed Dogmatics*, vol. 3: Christology, trans. by Richard B. Gaffin, Jr. (Lexham Press, 2012-2014), 3:80-81.

7 It is beyond the scope of this book to develop all the intricacies of trinitarian dogma. For a more detailed analysis of eternal generation of the Son and eternal spiration of the Holy Spirit, see: Francis Turretin, *Institutes of Elenctic Theology*, vol. 1, ed. by James T. Dennison, Jr., trans. by George Musgrave Giger (P&R, 1992), 1:253-310; Herman Bavinck, *Reformed Dogmatics: God and Creation*, vol. 2, ed. by John Bolt, trans. by John Vriend (Grand Rapids, MI: Baker Academic, 2004), 2:256-336; Vos, *Reformed Dogmatics*, 1:38-76.

8 "Father and the Son are related to one another within the personal context of God the Holy Spirit; the Father and the Spirit are related to one another within the personal context of God the Son; and the Son and the Spirit are related to one another within the personal context of God the Father." B. A. Bosserman, *The Trinity and the Vindication of Christian Paradox: An Interpretation and Refinement of the Theological Apologetic of Cornelius Van Til* (Pickwick, 2014), 178.

9 As quoted in: Calvin, *The Institutes of the Christian Religion*, I.13.17.

10 Bavinck, *Reformed Dogmatics*, 2:256-336; James R. White, *The Forgotten Trinity: Recovering the Heart of Christian Belief* (Bethany House, 1998); See also: https://www.monergism.com/thethreshold/sdg/Trinitarian%20Heresies.html.

11 Meaning "universal," rather than "the Roman Catholic Church."

12 The creed continues to discuss the incarnation. See: "The Athanasian Creed," in Liturgical Forms and Prayers of the United Reformed Churches in Northern America Together with the Doctrinal Standards of the URCNA (The United Reformed Churches in North America [Canada], 2018), 150-151.

[13] Oliphint, *The Majesty of Mystery*, 47.

[14] For exegesis of the 1 Corinthians 11:3 text, see: D. Glenn Butner. Jr., *The Son Who Learned Obedience: A Theological Case Against the Eternal Submission of the Son* (Pickwick, 2018), 185-189.

[15] Butner, *The Son Who Learned Obedience*, 194; cf. Bavinck, *Reformed Dogmatics*, 2:300.

[16] Mark Jones, *Knowing Christ* (The Banner of Truth Trust, 2015), 53-61, 63, 140.

[17] See: Butner, *The Son Who Learned Obedience*. Carlton Wynne helps to bring clarity to this issue and how it relates to the covenant of redemption (*pactum salutis*). See: Carl Trueman, "A Guest Post by Carlton Wynne," *Reformation 21*; June 16, 2016, https://www.reformation21.org/mos/postcards-from-palookaville/a-guest-post-by-carlton-wynne.

[18] Cornelius Van Til, *The Defense of the Faith*, 4th ed. ed. by K. Scott Oliphint (P&R, 2008), 34; also see: K. Scott Oliphint., "Cornelius Van Til and the Reformation of Christian Apologetics," in *Revelation and Reason: New Essays in Reformed Apologetics*, ed. by K. Scott Oliphint and Lane G. Tipton (P&R, 2007), 292-293.

[19] "The three persons of the Trinity know themselves truly and exhaustively not by way of direct self-reflection, but by beholding each of the two additional persons, through the mediation of the other. If God expresses himself exhaustively within the dynamic between divine persons from whom he is fundamentally different, it follows that he ought to be able to impart a finite knowledge of himself to man through created analogues that are wholly subject to his sovereign governance." Bosserman, *The Trinity and the Vindication of Christian Paradox*, 217. See also: Vern S. Poythress, *Knowing and the Trinity: How Perspectives in Human Knowledge Imitate the Trinity* (P&R, 2018); Vern S. Poythress, *Redeeming Philosophy: A God-Centered Approach to the Big Questions* (Crossway, 2014), 57-59, 120-126, 133, 142, 169, 182, 203, 269-276.

[20] Poythress, *Redeeming Philosophy*, 120.

[21] Francis A. Schaeffer, *He is There and He is Not Silent: Does it Make Sense to Believe in God?* (Tyndale House, 1972), 55-59.

[22] Van Til, *The Defense of the Faith*, 48.

[23] John M. Frame, *A History of Western Philosophy and Theology* (P&R, 2015), 532. See also: Vern S. Poythress, *Redeeming Philosophy: A God-Centered Approach to the Big Questions* (Crossway, 2014), 57-59, 120-126, 133, 142, 169, 182, 203, 269-276

[24] "Holy, Holy, Holy!" by Reginald Heber, in the Trinity Psalter Hymnal (Committee on Christian Education of the Orthodox Presbyterian Church and the Board of Directors of the United Reformed Churches in North America [USA], 2018), 230.

Chapter 8

[1] Cornelius Van Til, *Common Grace and the Gospel*, 2nd ed., ed. by K. Scott Oliphint (P&R, 2015), 216.

[2] Derek W. H. Thomas, *Acts*, Reformed Expository Commentary (P&R, 2011), 18.

[3] Gaffin said, "Involved here is, as it could be put, the 'mysterious math' of God's covenant, of his relationship, restored in Christ, between the Creator and his image-bearing creature, whereby 100% + 100% = 100%. Sanctification is 100 percent the work of God and, just for that reason, it is to engage 100 percent of the activity of the believer." Richard B. Gaffin, Jr., *By Faith, Not by Sight: Paul and the Order of Salvation*, 2nd ed. (P&R, 2013), 83.

[4] Proverbs 1:5; 4:5, 22; 7:4-5; 8:19, 32.

[5] Douglas Sean O'Donnell, *Ecclesiastes*, Reformed Expository Commentary (P&R, 2014), 40-41.

[6] See: Joel Beeke, *The Epistles of John* (EP Books, 2006), 136-140.

[7] Thomas Watson unpacks six ingredients of repentance: (1) sight of sin (Ps 51:3; Acts 26:18), (2) sorrow for sin (Ps 38:18; Zech 12:10), (3) confession of sin (Neh 9:2; Hos 5:15), (4) shame for sin (Ezra 9:6; Ezek 43:10), (5) hatred of sin (Ps 119:104; Ezek 36:31; Rom 7:15), (6) turning from sin (Isa 55:7; Ezek 14:6; Joel 2:12; Acts 26:20). Thomas Watson, *The Doctrine of Repentance*, Puritan Paperback (1668; Banner of Truth, 2016), 18-58.

[8] Good works are the necessary fruit of salvation. A person is not saved by good works, but he or she is not saved without them. They are the necessary consequence of regeneration and union with Christ. "Reformed theologians insisted good works, prepared in advance by God (Eph. 2:10) and done in the power of the Spirit (Rom. 9:9-14), are consequent conditions for salvation.... justification apart from the law and good works as necessary for salvation can stand together." Mark Jones, *Antinomianism: Reformed Theology's Unwelcome Guest?* (P&R, 2013), 64, 67-68.

[9] For a biblical understanding of the sin of homosexuality, see: Kevin DeYoung, *What Does the Bible Really Teach About Homosexuality?* (Crossway, 2015); Kevin Carson, "'Jason' and Homosexuality," in *Counseling the Hard Cases: True Stories Illustrating the Sufficiency of God's Resources in Scripture*, ed. by Stuart Scott and Heath Lambert (B&H, 2012), 227-255; Jay E. Adams, *The Christian Counselor's Manual: The Practice of Nouthetic Counseling* (Zondervan, 1973), 403-412.

[10] Beeke, *The Epistles of John*, 137

[11] John Owen, *The Mortification of Sin*, Puritan Paperbacks, ed. by Richard Rushing (Banner of Truth, 2009), 5. Owen goes on to say, "There is not a day but sin foils or is foiled, prevails or is prevailed upon. It will always be so while we live in this world. Sin will not spare for one day. There is no safety but in a constant warfare for those who desire deliverance from sin's perplexing rebellion," 7-8.

[12] See: Cornelius Van Til, *Common Grace and the Gospel*, 2nd ed., ed. by K. Scott Oliphint (P&R, 2015).

[13] See: Collin Hansen and D. A. Carson, "Does God Love the Sinner but Hate the Sin?", The TGC Podcast, The Gospel Coalition (10 November 2015), https://www.tgc.org/podcasts/tgc-podcast/does-god-love-the-sinner-but-hate-the-sin/.

[14] There is still a sense in which God loves His enemies. See: Van Til, *Common Grace and the Gospel,* 192-193.

[15] John Piper, "God Loves Sinners, but Hates the Sin?", Ask Pastor John, Desiring God (30 July 2013), https://www.desiringgod.org/interviews/god-loves-the-sinner-but-hates-the-sin.

[16] "He hates—now here is the paradox—and he loves at the same time. For God so loved the world that he hates. Hate and love are simultaneous as God looks upon hateful, rebellious, corrupt, loathsome, wicked, God-dishonoring sinners.... If we don't understand that God finds us hateful and loathsome in our ugly sin, we won't be as stunned by what love is for us. God saves millions of people who in and of themselves are loathsome to him until he saves them and makes them the apple of his eye." Piper, "God Loves Sinners, but Hates the Sin?"

[17] Deut 7:13; 11:14; 33:28; Judges 9:13; Neh 8:10-12; Ps 104:14-15; Prov 3:10; Eccl 9:7; Isa 55:1-3; Amos 9:14.

[18] Deut 28:51; Isa 62:8; Lam 2:12; Hag 1:10-11

[19] For more discussion on "good and necessary consequence," see: K. Scott Oliphint, "Because It Is the Word of God," in *Did God Really Say? Affirming the Truthfulness and Trustworthiness of Scripture,* ed. by David B. Garner (P&R, 2012), 9-11.

[20] I take the "one who eats" statement in v.3 as a synecdoche for the fuller statement in v.21, "eat meat, or drink wine, or do anything that makes your brother stumble."

[21] "Gracious Spirit, Dwell with Me," by Thomas T. Lynch, in the Trinity Psalter Hymnal (Committee on Christian Education of the Orthodox Presbyterian Church and the Board of Directors of the United Reformed Churches in North America [USA], 2018), 400.

Chapter 9

[1] Cornelius Van Til, *Common Grace and the Gospel,* 2nd ed., ed by K. Scott Oliphint (P&R, 2015), 191.

[2] John Calvin, *The Institutes of the Christian Religion,* vol. 2, trans. by Ford Lewis Battles, ed. by John T. McNeill (Westminster John Knox, 1960), III.21.3

[3] Joel Beeke describes Calvin's view of prayer: "[P]rayer allows the believer to appeal to the providence, predestination, omnipotence, and omniscience of God the Father. Prayer calls down the Father's tender mercy and care for His children because, having prayed, we have a sense of peace that God knows all and that He 'has both the will and the power to take the best care of us.' ... Our prayers do not get in the way of providence because God, in His providence, ordains the means along with the end. Prayer is thus a means ordained to receive what God has planned to bestow." Joel R. Beeke and Brian G. Najapfour, *Taking Hold of God: Reformed and Puritan Perspectives on Prayer* (Reformation Heritage, 2011), 29-30.

[4] Herman Witsius, *Sacred Dissertations on The Lord's Prayer*, trans. by William Pringle (1839; P&R, 1994), 46.

[5] For a defense of limited atonement, see: David Gibson and Jonathan Gibson, eds., *From Heaven He Came and Sought Her: Definite Atonement in Historical, Biblical, Theological, and Pastoral Perspectives* (Crossway, 2013).

[6] As quoted in: Patrick McIntyre, *The Graham Formula: Why Most Decisions for Christ are Ineffective* (White Harvest, 2005), 34.

[7] Cor Harinck, "Preparationism as Taught by the Puritans," *Puritan Reformed Journal* 2, no. 2 (2010), 164. I am reminded of Hopeful praying ten times before God saved him; see: John Bunyan, *The Pilgrim's Progress* (Answers in Genesis, 2006), 246-249. Also see: Rev. Robert Maguire, *Commentary on John Bunyan's the Pilgrim's Progress* (Curiosmith, 2009), 108-116.

[8] Charles Haddon Spurgeon wrote, "When I was coming to Christ, I thought I was doing it all myself, and though I sought the Lord earnestly, I had no idea the Lord was seeking me. I do not think the young convert is at first aware of this.... One weeknight, when I was sitting in the house of God, I was not thinking much about the preacher's sermon, for I did not believe it. The thought struck me, *How did you come to be a Christian?* I sought the Lord. *But how did you come to seek the Lord?* The truth flashed across my mind in a moment — I should not have sought Him unless there had been some previous influence in my mind to make me seek Him. I prayed, thought I, but then I asked myself, *How came I to pray?* I was induced to pray by reading the Scriptures. *How came I to read the Scriptures?* I did read them, but what led me to do so? Then, in a moment, I saw that God was at the bottom of it all, and that He was the Author of my faith, and so the whole doctrine of grace opened up to me, and from that doctrine I have not departed to this day, and I desire to make this my constant confession, 'I ascribe my change wholly to God.'" Charles Haddon Spurgeon, "A Defense of Calvinism," in *The Five Points of Calvinism: Defined, Defended, and Documented* by David N. Steele, Curtis C. Thomas, and S. Lance Quinn, 2nd ed. (P&R, 2004), 171-172. For more on the Puritan doctrine of "preparatory grace," see: Joel R. Beeke and Mark Jones, *A Puritan Theology: Doctrine for Life* (Reformation Heritage, 2012), 443-462.

[9] Heinrich Dezinger, *Compendium of Creeds, Definitions, and Declarations on Matters of Faith and Morals*, ed. by Peter Hünermann, 43rd edition (Ignatius Press, 2010), 134-136, 139.

[10] Though this passage is speaking about God's foreloving actions in Christ toward the elect, His foreknowledge could never be used to suppress His sovereignty, for "His foreknowledge is but a transcript of His will as to what shall come to pass in the future, and the course which the world takes under His providential control is but the execution of His all-embracing plan." Loraine Boettner, *The Reformed Doctrine of Predestination* (P&R, 1932), 99.

[11] John Piper, *Five Points: Towards a Deeper Experience of God's Grace* (Christian Focus, 2013), 53.

[12] Calvin says, "We are all lost in Adam; and therefore, had not God, through his own election, rescued us from perishing, there was nothing to be foreseen." John Calvin, *Epistle to the Ephesians*, in Calvin's Commentaries, vol. XXI (Baker, 2009), 198.

[13] John Murray, *The Epistle to the Romans*, vol. 1 (Eerdmans, 1959, 1965), 1:316-18.

[14] Douglas J. Moo, *The Letter to the Romans*, 2nd ed., New International Commentary on the New Testament (William B. Eerdmans, 2018), 554-555.

[15] Calvin, commenting on Ephesians 1:4-6, notes the three causes of our salvation: "The efficient cause is *the good pleasure of the will* of God, the material cause is, *Jesus Christ*, and the final cause is, *the praise of the glory of his grace.*" Calvin, *Epistle to the Ephesians*, 200, emphasis original.

[16] Greg Forster, *The Joy of Calvinism: Knowing God's Personal, Unconditional, Irresistible, Unbreakable Love* (Crossway, 2012), 84.

[17] "We shall never be clearly persuaded, as we ought to be, that our salvation flows from the wellspring of God's free mercy until we come to know his eternal election, which illumines God's grace by this contrast: that he does not indiscriminately adopt all into the hope of salvation but gives to some what he denies to others." Calvin, *The Institutes of the Christian Religion*, II.21.1.

[18] The Westminster Confession of Faith in the Trinity Psalter Hymnal (Committee on Christian Education of the Orthodox Presbyterian Church and the Board of Directors of the United Reformed Churches in North America [USA], 2018), 921-922.

[19] For more on the doctrines of grace, see: Matthew Barrett and Thomas J. Nettles, *Whomever He Wills: A Surprising Display of Sovereign Mercy* (Founders, 2012); Michael Horton, *For Calvinism* (Zondervan, 2011); John Piper, *Five Points: Towards a Deeper Experience of God's Grace* (Christian Focus, 2013); Benjamin B. Warfield, *The Plan of Salvation* (Simpson, 1989).

[20] "Abstract reasoning is inherently *nonhistorical* and thus nonbiblical. It moves the Arminian, as it does the unbeliever... toward a conclusion that negates Scripture's view of man and of history. And this is just to say that *concrete* thinking takes seriously the self-sufficiency (and meticulous sovereignty) of God, even while, at the same time, it affirms the meaningful progress of history and the real, meaningful, contingent, responsible choices of man." K. Scott Oliphint, "Introduction," in Cornelius Van Til, *Common Grace and the Gospel*, 2nd ed., ed. by K. Scott Oliphint (P&R, 2015), xxvii.

[21] Cotton Mather, *On Witchcraft* (1692; reprint, Dover, 2005), 25-26.

[22] Joel R. Beeke and Randall J. Pederson, *Meet the Puritans* (Reformation Heritage, 2006), 426.

[23] The Westminster Shorter Catechism, in the Trinity Psalter Hymnal, 970-971.

[24] "God Moves in a Mysterious Way," by William Cowper, in the Trinity Psalter Hymnal, 256.

Chapter 10

[1] I am thankful for my friends and classmates at Westminster Theological Seminary for bringing this analogy to my attention in our discussions.

[2] "When the apparently contradictory appears, as it always must when man seeks to know the relation of God to himself, there will be no denial of concepts such as election or human responsibility in the name of the law of contradiction." Cornelius Van Til, *Common Grace and the Gospel*, 2nd ed., ed. by K. Scott Oliphint (P&R, 2015), 232.

[3] J. Brandon Burks, *Internalizing the Faith: A Pilgrim's Catechism* (Fontes Press, 2018), 49; Cornelius Van Til, *The Defense of the Faith*, 4th ed., ed. by K. Scott Oliphint (P&R, 2008), 71, n.46.

[4] Van Til, *Common Grace and the Gospel*, 17.

[5] For a great discussion on compatibilism, see: D. A. Carson, *How Long O Lord? Reflections on Suffering and Evil*, 2nd ed. (Baker Academic, 2006), 177-204.

[6] The London Baptist Confession of Faith of 1689, in the Trinity Hymnal: Baptist Edition (Great Commission Publications, 1995), 672.

[7] Witsius said, "Our consciousness of freedom is so complete that to call it in question would be to dethrone reason itself. And yet, such is the wisdom and power of our God that, without any violation of that freedom, he can control the will according to his pleasure. He has his own secret entrance to the will, and acts upon it with a power which cannot be resisted, but with a power which makes it willing, and which, therefore, instead of injuring, declares, confirms, and maintains the freedom of the will. The will of God could not be done in all things, unless the fulfilment of his pleasure on our minds were within the reach of his power." Herman Witsius, *Sacred Dissertations on The Lord's Prayer*, trans. by William Pringle (1839; P&R, 1994), 264-265.

[8] John Frame, "The Problem of Evil," in *Suffering and the Goodness of God*, ed. Christopher W. Morgan and Robert A. Peterson (Crossway, 2008), 149.

[9] Charles Spurgeon, "Sovereign Grace and Man's Responsibility," *The Spurgeon Archive*, 1 August, 1858, http://archive.spurgeon.org/sermons/0207.php.

[10] "Man acts just as freely and just as guilty as if there were no predestination whatever. And God ordains, arranges, supervises, and overrules just as accurately as if there were no free will in the universe. Some people only believe one or the other of these two truths, yet they are both true, and the one is as true as the other.... The fault lies in trying to compress all truth of God under either of those two heads." Charles Spurgeon, study note on Gen 45:5, in *The Spurgeon Study Bible, CSB* (Holman, 2017), 64.

[11] Van Til, *Common Grace and the Gospel*, 17 n.42.

[12] For more on election and reprobation, see: Herman Bavinck, *Reformed Dogmatics: God and Creation*, vol. 2, ed. by John Bolt, trans. by John Vriend (Baker, 2004), 2:337-405; Joel R. Beeke and Mark Jones, *A Puritan Theology: Doctrine for Life* (Reformation Heritage, 2012), 117-132; Van Til, *Common Grace and the Gospel*, 157-167; Robert Letham, *Systematic Theology* (Crossway, 2019), 405-439.

[13] Daniel B. Wallace, *Greek Grammar Beyond the Basics: An Exegetical Syntax of the New Testament* (Zondervan, 1996), 101, 417-418.

[14] Article 16 of the Belgic Confession reads, "We believe that—all Adam's descendants having thus fallen into perdition and ruin by the sin of Adam—God showed himself to be as he is: merciful and just. God is merciful in withdrawing and saving from this perdition those who, in the eternal and unchangeable divine counsel, have been elected and chosen in Jesus Christ our Lord by his pure goodness, without any consideration of their works. God is just in leaving the others in their ruin and fall into which they plunged themselves." In the Trinity Psalter Hymnal (Committee on Christian Education of the Orthodox Presbyterian Church and the Board of Directors of the United Reformed Churches in North America [USA], 2018), 860-861.

[15] Douglas Moo says, "Paul appropriately concludes one of his most profound and difficult theological discussions with a hymn in praise of God for his purposes and plans.... We should, then, perhaps understand Paul's praise to be motivated not so much by the hiddenness of God's ways but by the (admittedly partial) revelation of those mind-transcending ways to us." Douglas J. Moo, *The Letter to the Romans*, 2nd ed., New International Commentary on the New Testament (William B. Eerdmans, 2018), 759.

[16] Carl Trueman said it well: "In Christ he [God] sets forth his merciful intentions in such a way that none who come to him by faith will be cast aside. Yes, it is true that the decree of predestination is still there in the background, but the great promises of God's bounteous grace, linked to his saving action in Christ, give full grounds and confidence for believing that any who look to him for salvation will be saved." Carl Trueman, *Grace Alone: Salvation as a Gift of God* (Zondervan, 2017), 147-148.

[17] The Canons of Dort, The Third and Fourth Main Points of Doctrine, Articles 8-9, in the Trinity Psalter Hymnal, 907-908.

[18] Every person who believes will be saved. But why do some believe and not others? Orrick explains, "We did not choose him because we were more spiritually minded than someone else. We did not choose him because we were intelligent enough to see it was the right thing to do. We were part of the world that 'did not know God through wisdom' (1 Cor. 1:21). Jesus said, 'You did not choose me, but I chose you' (John 15:16). The doctrine of unconditional election ought to cultivate the deepest humiliation in us and provoke the highest praise from us." Jim Scott Orrick, *Mere Calvinism* (P&R, 2019), 66-67.

[19] "We Praise You and Acknowledge You, O God" by Stephen P. Starke (Concordia Publishing House, 1999), https://stpaulsfw.org/images/weeks-message/hymn-text/LSB-941-We-Praise-You-and-Acknowledge-You-O-Lord.pdf.

[20] "Sovereign Ruler of the Skies," by John Ryland (1777), https://founders.org/2016/06/14/hymns-and-the-doctrine-of-election/.

[21] "Lord, My Weak Thought in Vain Would Climb," by Ray Palmer, in the Trinity Psalter Hymnal, 225.

Chapter 11

[1] R. C. Sproul, *Chosen By God: Knowing God's Perfect Plan for His Glory and His Children* (Tyndale House, 1986), 17-27.

[2] "What peculiarly tends to illustrate and recommend to us the eternal and unmerited grace of election, is the express testimony of sacred Scripture, that not all, but some only are elected, while others are passed by in the eternal election of God; whom God, out of his sovereign, most just, irreprehensible and unchangeable good pleasure, hath decreed to leave in the common misery into which they have willfully plunged themselves, and not to bestow upon them saving faith and the grace of conversion; but leaving them in his just judgment to follow their own ways, at last for the declaration of his justice, to condemn and punish them forever, not only on account of their unbelief, but also for all their other sins. And this is the decree of reprobation which by no means makes God the author of sin (the very thought of which is blasphemy), but declares him to be an awful, irreprehensible, and righteous judge and avenger thereof." Canons of Dort, First Head of Doctrine, Article 15, in the Trinity Psalter Hymnal (Committee on Christian Education of the Orthodox Presbyterian Church and the Board of Directors of the United Reformed Churches in North America [USA], 2018), 909.

[3] Vermigli says, "Although sins are in one sense subject to the will of God, they are not produced by it in the same way as are good deeds. Yet it should be certain that sins are not done completely apart from any will of God. 'Permission,' which some acknowledge, is no different from will, for God permits what he will not prevent. Nor should it be said that he permits unwillingly, but willingly, as Augustine said." Peter Martyr Vermigli, *Predestination and Justification: Two Theological Loci*, trans. and ed. by Frank A. James III, in Sixteenth Century Essays and Studies, vol. LXVIII (The Davenant Press, 2018), 73.

[4] D. A. Carson, *How Long O Lord? Reflections on Suffering and Evil*, 2nd ed. (Baker Academic, 2006), 189.

[5] John MacArthur, *The MacArthur Daily Bible: New King James Version* (Thomas Nelson, 2003), 88.

[6] "The apostle Paul used this hardening as an example of God's inscrutable will and absolute power to intervene as He chooses, yet obviously never without loss of personal responsibility for actions taken. The theological conundrum posed by such interplay of God's acting and Pharaoh's acting can only be resolved by accepting the record as it stands and by taking refuge in the omniscience and omnipotence of the God who planned and brought about His deliverance of Israel from Egypt and, in so doing, also judged Pharaoh's sinfulness." Ibid.

[7] Cornelius Van Til, *Common Grace and the Gospel*, 2nd ed., ed. by K. Scott Oliphint (P&R, 2015), 82-83.

[8] "The word 'concursus' is a Latin term that means 'to run together.'.... God is the original, or first, cause of any choice that we make, and a person is the second, or dependent,

cause of that choice. When we choose something, there is a concursus taking place, in that God has ordained and caused that choice, but we also really and responsibly choose. God causes first, but is not responsible for what we choose. Then, concurrent to God's cause, we choose and are, thus, secondary causes. But how can there be a first and a second cause involved in my choice, and only the second one be *responsible* for it? Herein lies the mystery." K. Scott Oliphint, *The Majesty of Mystery: Celebrating the Glory of an Incomprehensible God* (Lexham Press, 2016), 155.

[9] See: Brian H. Cosby, *Suffering and Sovereignty: John Flavel and the Puritans on Afflictive Providence* (Reformation Trust, 2012).

[10] R. C. Sproul, *What is Reformed Theology? Understanding the Basics* (Baker: 1997), 108; Also see: Mark Jones, *Knowing Christ* (The Banner of Truth Trust, 2015), 9.

[11] Van Til, *Common Grace and the Gospel*, 166-167.

[12] "Before there was any human sin to die for, God planned that his Son be slain for sinners. We know this because of the name given to the book of life before creation. 'Everyone [will worship the beast] whose name has not been written before the foundation of the world in *the book of life of the Lamb who was slain*' (Revelation 13:8). The name of the book before creation was 'the book of life of the Lamb who was slain.' The plan was glory. The plan was grace. The plan was Christ. And the plan was death. And that death for sinners like us is the heart of the gospel, which is why in 2 Corinthians 4:4 Paul calls it 'the gospel of the glory of God'." John Piper, *Doctrine Matters: Ten Theological Trademarks from a Lifetime of Preaching* (Desiring God, 2013), 32; cf. 29-40.

[13] "Therefore, although John wrote in cloaked language, it would have been clear to the first recipients of this book that he referred to the idolatrous political and religious systems by which Satan attacked the church through the civic and cultural institutions of the world." Joel R. Beeke, *Revelation*, The Lectio Continua Expository Commentary on the New Testament, ed. by Joel R. Beeke and Jon D. Payne (RHB, 2016), 363. Also see: G. K. Beale, *The Book of Revelation*, The New International Greek Testament Commentary, ed. by I. Howard Marshall and Donald A. Hagner (William B. Eerdmans, 1999), 686-688; Richard D. Phillips, *Revelation*, Reformed Expository Commentary (P&R, 2017), 177, 286.

[14] Van Til, *Common Grace and the Gospel*, 82.

[15] "A Mighty Fortress Is Our God," by Martin Luther, trans. by Frederick H. Hedge, in the Trinity Psalter Hymnal, 244.

Chapter 12

[1] Vermigli provides further nuance to the 'wills of God' discussion: Peter Martyr Vermigli, *Predestination and Justification: Two Theological Loci*, trans. and ed. by Frank A. James III, in Sixteenth Century Essays and Studies, vol. LXVIII (The Davenant Press, 2018), 45-47, 62-74.

[2] The Westminster Shorter Catechism in the Trinity Psalter Hymnal (Committee on Christian Education of the Orthodox Presbyterian Church and the Board of Directors of the United Reformed Churches in North America [USA], 2018), 970-971.

[3] The Belgic Confession, in the Trinity Psalter Hymnal, 856.

[4] Martin Luther, *The Bondage of the Will*, trans. by J. I. Packer and O. R. Johnston (Baker, 1957), 169-170.

[5] Witsuis said, "The will of God must therefore be viewed in a twofold aspect; First, as it denotes the DECREE or *purpose of God*, by which he determined, in his own mind, from all eternity, what would take place, in time, for his own glory.... *Secondly*, as it denotes the COMMANDMENT of God, by which he binds his rational creatures to obedience. This will points out what ought to be done, but does not determine what shall actually take place.... The one will is the cause of all that is done; the other is the rule of what ought to be done. Both belong to God as most absolute king and Lord, and are founded on his boundless power, and on his other perfections and excellencies." Herman Witsius, *Sacred Dissertations on The Lord's Prayer*, trans. by William Pringle (1839; P&R, 1994), 251. Also see: John Piper, "How to Know the Will of God: Finding Direction with the Renewed Mind," sermon, Good Shepherd Community Church, (September 27, 2015), https://www.desiringgod.org/messages/how-to-know-the-will-of-god.

[6] "In affirming this, however, we also should recognize that God's own intent in His 'secret' will is of a different kind, or mode, than His 'revealed' will. What God wills in eternity necessarily happens. His will in eternity ordains 'whatsoever comes to pass.' But His will, or desire, as He expresses it... is not an ordaining will or desire. Instead, it is God expressing His desire that what He has commanded of us would be carried out by us all." K. Scott Oliphint, *The Majesty of Mystery: Celebrating the Glory of an Incomprehensible God* (Lexham Press, 2016), 135.

[7] Herman Bavinck, *Reformed Dogmatics: Abridged in One Volume*, ed. by John Bolt (Baker Academics, 2011), 212; see also: Francis Turretin, *Institutes of Elenctic Theology*, vol. 1, trans. by George Musgrave Giger, ed. by James T. Dennison, Jr. (P&R, 1992), 220-222, 228-231.

[8] "[T]he will of decree may be that which determines the event of things, but the will of precept that which prescribes to man his duty. Therefore God can (without contradiction) will as to precept what he does not will as to decree inasmuch as he wills to prescribe something to man, but does not will to effect it (as he willed Pharaoh to release the people, but yet nilled their actual release)." Turretin, *Institutes,* 1:221.

[9] Oliphint, *The Majesty of Mystery,* 136-137.

[10] "For the physician uses not only ointments but fire and iron, with which he cuts and burns away whatever is superfluous and brings healing by the wound he causes. He removes anything which would prevent the ointment from healing. In the same way, God, the physician of souls, brings... tribulations. And when it is afflicted and humiliated by these its joy turns to sorrow (Bar 4:34; Jas 4:9). It thinks what has been revealed

to it is an illusion. So it comes to be free of vanity and the truth of revelation endures. Thus was Paul's pride kept in check by the stings of the flesh, through he himself was lifted up by many revelations (2 Cor 12:7)." St. Bernard, *Bernard of Clairvaux: Selected Works*, in The Classics of Western Spirituality, trans. by G. R. Evans (Paulist Press, 1987), 130.

[11] See: Piper, "How to Know the Will of God."

[12] If you push God away, "You will now be left with no God to help you deal with this and turn it [for] good. He will be useless. You have just shoved him off into a realm where he can't have anything to do with what happened.... If he can't govern that moment, [then] he can't govern the rest of your life and do the miracles [that] you need for him to do. So you need two things.... [First, you need] a God who can empathize with you as a high priest [who] hates sin. The definition of sin is God hates it and says, 'Don't do it! I forbid it.' And you need a God in that moment who is totally sovereign and governing all things so that even the sin being done against you is folded into his purposes for you and you can shine like the sun someday even in spite of that loss, that pain. Both of those are needs that I think God meets by being this kind of God." Ibid.

[13] John Piper, *Desiring God: Meditations of a Christian Hedonist*, rev. ed. (Multnomah, 2011), 39.

[14] See: Luther, *The Bondage of the Will*, 202-203.

[15] G. K. Beale, *1-2 Thessalonians*, IVP New Testament Commentary, ed. by Grant R. Osborne (IVP, 2003), 171.

[16] Brian H. Cosby, *Suffering and Sovereignty: John Flavel and the Puritans on Afflictive Providence* (Reformation Trust, 2012), 101-105.

[17] Thomas Watson, *All Things for Good*, Puritan Paperbacks (1663; Banner of Truth, 1986; reprint 2013).

[18] "I Greet Thee, Who My Sure Redeemer Art," by John Calvin, trans. by Elizabeth Lee Smith, in the Trinity Psalter Hymnal (Committee on Christian Education of the Orthodox Presbyterian Church and the Board of Directors of the United Reformed Churches in North America [USA], 2018), 282.

Chapter 13

[1] Timothy Brindle, *The Unfolding* (Lamp Mode Publishing, 2017), 7.

[2] Ibid. Reformed Baptists and Presbyterians disagree on the natures of the Old and New Covenants. Nevertheless, Reformed Baptists would agree with Brindle on the progressive unfolding of the promised Messiah from Genesis to Revelation. For a Reformed Baptist understanding, see: Samuel Renihan, *The Mystery of Christ: His Covenant and His Kingdom* (Founders, 2019). For a more Reformed/Presbyterian understanding, see: Michael Horton, *God of Promise: Introducing Covenant Theology* (Baker, 2006).

[3] This is Meredith Kline's description of intrusion: "[W]ithin this temporary shell of the Intrusion there is a permanent core. The pattern of things earthly embodies realized eschatology, an actual projection of the heavenly reality. It is the consummation which, intruding into the time of delay, anticipates itself." Meredith G. Kline, *The Structures of Biblical Authority*, 2nd ed. (Wipf and Stock, 1989), 156.

[4] See: T. Desmond Alexander, *From Paradise to the Promised Land: An Introduction to the Pentateuch*, 3rd ed. (Baker Academic, 2012), 206-208.

[5] Kline, *The Structures of Biblical Authority*, 156.

[6] Ibid., 156-157.

[7] Ibid., 157, 162-164.

[8] See: G. K. Beale and David H. Campbell, *Revelation: A Shorter Commentary* (William B. Eerdmans, 2015), 412.

[9] Kline, *The Structures of Biblical Authority*, 163, 167.

[10] Regarding the Trumpet-calamity in Revelation chapter 8, Joel Beeke writes, "These judgments include economic, ecological, industrial, and physical disasters upon the earth. The apostle John teaches us that we are to listen to the voice of God in history, particularly to His judgments against sin. Furthermore, we must respond to them by repenting of our sins, unlike Pharaoh, whose heart clamped shut against God." Joel Beeke, *Revelation*, The Lectio Continua Expository Commentary on the New Testament (Reformation Heritage Books, 2016), 267.

[11] This analogy is from: David Murray, *Jesus on Every Page: Ten Simple Ways to Seek and Find Christ in the Old Testament* (Thomas Nelson, 2013), 105.

[12] To understand Pentecost and speaking in tongues, see: Richard B. Gaffin Jr., *Perspectives on Pentecost: New Testament Teaching on the Gifts of the Holy Spirit* (P&R, 1979).

[13] Geerhardus Vos, "The Eschatological Aspect of the Pauline Conception of the Spirit," in *Redemptive History and Biblical Interpretation: Shorter Writings of Geerhardus Vos*, ed. by Richard B. Gaffin, Jr. (P&R, 1980), 103.

[14] See: Murray, *Jesus on Every Page*, 87-88; Joseph A. Pipa, *The Lord's Day* (Christian Focus, 1997; reprint, 2008), 26-27; Renihan, *The Mystery of Christ*, 135-208.

[15] "O Come, O Come, Emmanuel," trans. John Mason Neale, in the Trinity Psalter Hymnal (Committee on Christian Education of the Orthodox Presbyterian Church and the Board of Directors of the United Reformed Churches in North America [USA], 2018), 293.

Chapter 14

[1] William L. Holladay, ed., *A Concise Hebrew and Aramaic Lexicon of the Old Testament* (William B. Eerdmans, 1988), 76.

[2] "We think. God gives. Both-and. Not either-or.... He emphatically makes God's gift of illumination the ground of our deliberation. He makes God's giving light the reason for our pursuing light." John Piper, *Reading the Bible Supernaturally: Seeing and Savoring the Glory of God in Scripture* (Crossway, 2017), 240.

[3] "Reading the Bible, in reliance on God, is one particular act among thousands of acts that, in the Christian life, are supernatural in this way." Ibid., 241.

[4] See: J. I. Packer, *Concise Theology: A Guide to Historic Christian Beliefs* (Tyndale House, 1993), 154-156; John Murray, *Collected Writings of John Murray*, vol. 1: The Claims of Truth (The Banner of Truth, 1976), 186-189.

[5] Charles Spurgeon exhorted his congregation, "Ah, beloved, let us thank God for this Bible; let us love it; let us count it more precious than much fine gold.... If this be the Word of God, what will become of some of you who have not read it for the last month? 'Month, sir! I have not read it for this year.' Ay, there are some of you who have not read it at all. Most people treat the Bible very politely. They have a small pocket volume, neatly bound; they put a white pocket-handkerchief round it and carry it to their places of worship; when they get home, they lay it up in a drawer till next Sunday morning; then it comes out again for a little bit of a treat, and goes to chapel; that is all the poor Bible gets in the way of an airing. That is your style of entertaining this heavenly messenger. There is dust enough on some of your Bibles to write 'damnation' with your fingers. There are some of you who have not turned over your Bibles for a long, long while, and what think you? I tell you blunt words. What will God say at last? When you shall come before him, he shall say, 'Did you read my Bible?' 'No.' 'I wrote you a letter of mercy; did you read it?' 'No.' 'Rebel! I have sent thee a letter inviting thee to me; didst thou ever read it?' '*Lord, I never broke the seal; I kept it shut up,*' 'Wretch!' says God, 'then, thou deserves hell, if I sent thee a loving epistle, and thou wouldst not even break the seal; what shall I do unto thee?' Oh, let it not be so with you. Be Bible-readers; be Bible-searchers" Charles Spurgeon, "The Bible," in *Spurgeon's Sermons*, vol. 1 (Hendrickson, 2011), 33-34.

[6] Joel R. Beeke and Mark Jones, *A Puritan Theology: Doctrine for Life* (Reformation Heritage, 2012), 889.

[7] Ibid., 894.

[8] Ibid.

[9] Herman Witsius, *Sacred Dissertations on The Lord's Prayer*, trans. by William Pringle (1839; P&R, 1994), 198.

[10] St. Chrysostom, *The Homilies On The Statues: To The People Of Antioch*, trans. by W. R. W. Stephens, ed. by Philip Schaff. (Christian Literature, 1889) 373, BibleWorks.

[11] "How Firm a Foundation," attr. to George Keith and R. Keen, in the Trinity Psalter Hymnal (Committee on Christian Education of the Orthodox Presbyterian Church and the Board of Directors of the United Reformed Churches in North America [USA], 2018), 243.

Chapter 15

[1] Vern S. Poythress, *Reading the Word of God in the Presence of God: A Handbook for Biblical Interpretation* (Crossway, 2016).

[2] John Piper, *Reading the Bible Supernaturally: Seeing and Savoring the Glory of God in Scripture* (Crossway, 2017).

[3] "The words of the Old Testament often contain more than the writers themselves understood." Richard B. Gaffin, Jr., *God's Word in Servant Form: Abraham Kuyper and Herman Bavinck on the Doctrine of Scripture* (Reformed Academic Press, 2008), 16. Indeed, the words or sentences written by the biblical authors "can have a much deeper meaning than the writer intended." Ibid., 61.

[4] Meaning "is like a stable particle. It remains the same through time. The idea of stability though time has its foundation in God, who is faithful and who remains the same through time. God knows the end from the beginning (Isa. 46:10). What he knows about what he means with a text and what he knows that he will do with the text throughout all of history is the same through all time." Poythress, *Reading the Word of God in the Presence of God*, 170.

[5] Edmund P. Clowney, *Preaching Christ in All of Scripture* (Crossway, 2003), 23.

[6] "Illumination coordinates with perspicuity because the Spirit of Truth illumines us to the resident and vital meaning of Scripture. We understand Scripture not because the Holy Spirit takes that which is opaque or translucent and makes it transparent; instead, we understand Scripture because the Holy Spirit transforms us, removing the moral blinders from our hearts' eyes and enabling us to see Scripture for what it is (cf. 2 Tim. 3:16-17; 2 Peter 1:19-21). Perspicuity provides the objective basis for illumination; illumination is not the basis for perspicuity.... Illumination does not change Scripture, it changes us." David Garner, "Did God Really Say?" in *Did God Really Say? Affirming the Truthfulness and Trustworthiness of Scripture*, ed. by David Garner (P&R, 2012), 152.

[7] The 1689 Baptist Confession of Faith, 1.9 says, "The infallible rule of interpretation of Scripture is the Scripture itself; and therefore when there is a question about the true and full sense of any Scripture (which is not manifold, but one), it must be searched by other places that speak more clearly. (2 Pet. 1:20-21; Acts 15:15-16)."

[8] Richard B. Gaffin, Jr., "Systematic Theology and Hermeneutics," in *Seeing Christ in All of Scripture: Hermeneutics at Westminster Theological Seminary*, ed. by Peter A. Lillback (WSP, 2016), 41.

[9] Here in the text we see an emphatic negation subjunctive, one of the strongest ways to negate something in Greek: "They will *not at all* perish." Daniel Wallace, *Greek Grammar Beyond the Basics: An Exegetical Syntax of the New Testament* (Zondervan, 1996), 468.

[10] The Reformed and Presbyterians make a distinction between a *covenant member* and a *born-again believer*. The Reformed Baptists do not; thus, Reformed Baptists will

also argue that Jeremiah seems to suggest that the nature of the New Covenant is such that its members do not fall away or commit apostasy (32:40).

[11] I find the first view, however, more persuasive.

[12] Robert A. Peterson and Michael D. Williams, *Why I Am Not an Arminian* (IVP, 2004), 84.

[13] Van Til said, "The real question is one of epistemology and therewith of man's ethical attitude toward God. If men were fully self-conscious epistemologically they would violently suppress the psychologically interpretative voice within them. But to the extent that they are not self-conscious epistemologically, they may even taste the heavenly gifts, be made partakers of the Holy Ghost, and taste the good word of God and the powers of the world to come, and not rebel (see Heb. 6:4-6). They allow themselves to be affected to some extent." Cornelius Van Til, *Common Grace and the Gospel*, 2nd ed., ed by K. Scott Oliphint (P&R, 2015), 103.

[14] John Murray, "Common Grace," in *Collected Writings of John Murray*, vol. 2: Systematic Theology (Banner of Truth, 1977; reprint, 2009), 110.

[15] Thomas R. Schreiner, *Run to Win the Prize: Perseverance in the New Testament* (Apollos, 2009), 46.

[16] Ibid., 50, 96.

[17] Timothy Brindle, *The Unfolding* (Lamp Mode Publishing, 2017), 15. Johannes Oecolampadius rightfully said, "Because the Word of God is inspired by the Holy Spirit, I am unable not to affirm that in all places the Spirit of the Scriptures has regard for Christ Jesus in purpose, goal, and method." Quoted in: Joel R. Beeke, *Reformed Preaching: Proclaiming God's Word from the Heart of the Preacher to the Heart of His People* (Crossway, 2018), 110.

[18] "The prophets sought out and carefully inquired about the salvation that had come to the Christians of Peter's Day. By pointing this out, Peter draws a continuity between what had been foretold in the OT and what was being realized in the life of Jesus and preached in the gospel. The Christians to whom Peter writes are not to understand themselves as practitioners of yet another new religion in the world, founded on the person of Jesus of Nazareth. Rather, they are being privileged with the knowledge of the gospel that fulfills God's mysterious plan as revealed to the prophets of the OT and that brings them into continuity with what God has already been doing through ancient Israel.... Peter views the gospel of Jesus Christ as one with the message of the OT." Karen H. Jobes, *1 Peter*, Baker Exegetical Commentaries (Baker Academics, 2005), 98.

[19] Lane G. Tipton, "The Gospel and Redemptive-Historical Hermeneutics," in *Confident of Better Things: Essays Commemorating Seventy-Five Years of the Orthodox Presbyterian Church*, ed. by John R. Meuther and Danny E. Olinger (The Committee for the Historian of the Orthodox Presbyterian Church, 2011), 187-188.

[20] Also see: G. K. Beale, "The Cognitive Peripheral Vision of Biblical Authors," Westminster Theological Journal 76:2 (Fall 2014): 263-9.

[21] Gaffin, Jr., *God's Word in Servant Form*, 17.

[22] "By quoting Hosea 11:1, Matthew taps directly into the whole of Hosea 11:1-11, which is marked by its realized-future Egypt typology with related allusions and associations within the overall context of Hosea.... The promised exodus-salvation of the sinful son-servant nation in view in Hosea 11:11, for which return from Assyrian exile was and could be only a pointer, will be accomplished by the messianic servant-son." Richard B. Gaffin, Jr., "The Redemptive-Historical View," in *Biblical Hermeneutics: Five Views*, ed. by Stanley E. Porter and Beth M. Stovell (IVP Academic, 2012), 107-108; cf. 102-110.

[23] David Murray, *Jesus on Every Page: Ten Simple Ways to Seek and Find Christ in the Old Testament* (Thomas Nelson, 2013), 138.

[24] Adam York, Camden Bucey, Matthew Patton, and Nick Batzig, "Typology and Jehoiachin," Christ the Center, Reformed Forum (7 June, 2013), https://reformedforum.org/ctc284/.

[25] See: Murray, *Jesus on Every Page*, 77-82.

[26] Paul likely read "Christ" wherever *kurios* (or "Lord") appeared in the LXX. Clowney, *Preaching Christ in All of Scripture*, 13. See also: K. Scott Oliphint, *The Majesty of Mystery: Celebrating the Glory of an Incomprehensible God* (Lexham Press, 2016), 59-110.

[27] See: Samuel Renihan, *The Mystery of Christ: His Covenant and His Kingdom* (Founders, 2019), 27-39.

[28] Beale discusses Revelation 1:1, writing, "The clause 'revelation... God showed... what must come to pass... and he *made known* (σημαίνω)' occur together only in Daniel 2 and Rev. 1:1. In the LXX of Daniel 2, σημαίνω is a translation of the Aramaic *yĕda'* ('make known'); Theod. has γνωρίζω ('make known'). Even with the more general terms in Aramaic and Theod., the manner of communication is defined by the context of the vision as symbolic communication by means of a dream vision. In the LXX the symbolic nature of communication is also signaled by the use of σημαίνω.... The symbolic use of σημαίνω in Daniel 2 defines the use in Rev. 1:1 as referring to symbolic communication and not mere general conveyance of information." G. K. Beale, *The Book of Revelation*, New International Greek Testament Commentary, ed. by I. Howard Marshall and Donald A. Hagner (William B. Eerdmans, 1999), 50-51; cf. 50-69.

[29] Robert L. Plummer, *40 Questions About Interpreting the Bible*, ed. by Benjamin L. Merkle (Kregel, 2010), 185-292.

[30] Vern S. Poythress, "Dispensing with Merely Human Meaning: Gains and Losses from Focusing on the Human Author, Illustrated by Zephaniah 1:2–3," *JETS* 57.3 (2014): 481–99.

[31] Vern S. Poythress, *Reading the Word of God in the Presence of God: A Handbook for Biblical Interpretation* (Crossway, 2016), 121, 127.

[32] Paul is specifically prohibiting women from teaching the Bible (doctrine; the message of Jesus) to men within the activities and ministries of the local church. See: William D. Mounce, *Pastoral Epistles*, Word Biblical Commentary, vol. 46, ed. by Bruce M. Metzger (Thomas Nelson, 2000), 125; Andreas J. Köstenberger and Thomas Schreiner, eds., *Women in the Church: An Interpretation and Application of 1 Timothy 2:9-15*, 3rd ed.

(Crossway, 2016), 190-195; Douglas J. Moo, "What Does it Mean Not to Teach or Have Authority Over Men? 1 Timothy 2:11-15," in *Recovering Biblical Manhood and Womanhood: A Response to Evangelical Feminism*, ed. by John Piper and Wayne Grudem (Crossway, 2006), 185-187.

[33] The Jews hated the Samaritans. See: David E. Garland, *Luke*, in Exegetical Commentary on the New Testament, ed. by Clinton E. Arnold (Zondervan, 2011), 443-444.

[34] Perhaps Jesus is not saying, "either love God or hate God," but rather, "be useful." Cold water is useful for drinking and hot water is useful for bathing. Lukewarm water just makes people sick, as the reader would have experienced in their local aqueduct system. See: Joel R. Beeke, *Revelation* (Reformation Heritage, 2016), 160-163.

[35] G. K. Beale, *A New Testament Biblical Theology: The Unfolding of the Old Testament in the New* (Baker Academic, 2011), 1-7.

[36] Ibid. I am also thankful for Lane Tipton, who drilled this truth into us in Doctrine of Salvation at Westminster Theological Seminary in the spring of 2017.

[37] A "main point" is the point that "everything else supports but it itself does not support anything in that unit." John Piper, *Reading the Bible Supernaturally: Seeing and Savoring the Glory of God in Scripture* (Crossway, 2017), 395.

[38] There are great resources for tracing the flow of the Author's argument to find the main point. Some people refer to this as *discourse analysis*, others call it *rhetorical analysis*, and others call it *arcing*. See: Piper, *Reading the Bible Supernaturally*, 365-411; Poythress, *Reading the Word of God in the Presence of God*, 197-206; G. K. Beale, Daniel J. Brendsel, and William A. Ross, *An Interpretive Lexicon of New Testament Greek: Analysis of Prepositions, Adverbs, Particles, Relative Pronouns, and Conjunctions* (Zondervan, 2014).

[39] "The implications of [desiring to find the author's meaning] are life changing. You will never go to the Bible again simply to see if you can feel inspired by whatever comes to your mind. You will never be content in a group Bible study where the aim is for everyone to say 'what the text means to you.' You will not be excited about a pastor who tells you interesting stories and talks about history and politics and psychology and personal experiences but never shows you what the biblical authors intended to communicate in particular texts... Instead you will make every effort to read the Bible in a way that opens the intentions of the authors and inspires you with *that*. You will seek to see and savor God through *that*. You will love small-group Bible studies where everyone is helping each other see aspects of the text that bring out more and more of what the author really meant. You will give God thanks for every sermon that shows you what the biblical authors actually meant. And, yes, in your personal reading and group study and sermon listening, you will seek to apply the meaning to your life and your circumstances and your world. And the power of that application will increase with the confidence that it is based on real, objective, unchanging meaning that is really there." Piper, *Reading the Bible Supernaturally*, 309-310.

[40] Clowney, *Preaching Christ in All of Scripture*, 32; Poythress, *Reading the Word of God in the Presence of God*, 245-262.

[41] Clowney, *Preaching Christ in All of Scripture*, 34.

[42] For the proper understanding of 1 Samuel 16-17, see: Brindle, *The Unfolding*, 83-109; see also: Clowney, *Preaching Christ in All of Scripture*, 34.

[43] Clowney, *Preaching Christ in All of Scripture*, 34.

[44] Brindle, *The Unfolding*, 83-109.

[45] Being victorious, however, does not mean Christians will never experience tribulation, martyrdom, and persecution. In fact, sometimes it is *through* martyrdom that Christians will be victorious. See: Phillips, *Revelation* (2017), 385; G. K. Beale, *The Book of Revelation*, 991; George Eldon Ladd, *A Commentary on the Revelation of John* (William B. Eerdmans, 1972), 116.

[46] "Eternal Is Your Word, O Lord," by John B. Dykes, in the Trinity Psalter Hymnal (Committee on Christian Education of the Orthodox Presbyterian Church and the Board of Directors of the United Reformed Churches in North America [USA], 2018), 119L.

Chapter 16

[1] Charles Hodge, *Systematic Theology*, vol. 1 (Hendrickson, 2008), 1:21.

[2] Geerhardus Vos, *Biblical Theology: Old and New Testaments* (The Banner of Truth, 2012), 4-5; Danny E. Olinger, *Geerhardus Vos: Reformed Biblical Theologian, Confessional Presbyterian* (Reformed Forum, 2018), 144; cf. 141-160.

[3] Helpful resources for Exegetical Theology include: William L. Holladay, ed., *A Concise Hebrew and Aramaic Lexicon of the Old Testament* (William B. Eerdmans, 1988); Frederick William Danker, ed., *A Greek-English Lexicon of the New Testament and Other Early Christian Literature*, 3rd ed. (University of Chicago Press, 2000); Daniel Wallace, *Greek Grammar Beyond the Basics: An Exegetical Syntax of the New Testament* (Zondervan, 1996); Bruce M. Metzger, *A Textual Commentary on the Greek New Testament*, 2nd ed. (United Bible Society, 1994); Philip Wesley Comfort, *A Commentary on the Manuscripts and Text of the New Testament* (Kregel, 2015); Robert L. Thomas, ed., *The Strongest NASB Exhaustive Concordance* (Zondervan, 1998); G. K. Beale, Daniel J. Brendsel, and William A. Ross, *An Interpretive Lexicon of New Testament Greek: Analysis of Prepositions, Adverbs, Particles, Relative Pronouns, and Conjunctions* (Zondervan, 2014); Chad Brand and Eric Mitchell, eds., *Holman Illustrated Bible Dictionary* (Holman Reference, 2015); G. K. Beale and D. A. Carson, eds., *Commentary on the New Testament Use of the Old Testament* (Baker Academic, 2007); Bruce M. Metzger and Bart D. Ehrman, *The Text of the New Testament: Its Transmission, Corruption, and Restoration*, 4th ed. (Oxford University Press, 2005).

[4] Vern S. Poythress, *Reading the Word of God in the Presence of God: A Handbook for Biblical Interpretation* (Crossway, 2016), 36.

[5] Resources for Biblical Theology include: Nancy Guthrie, *Even Better Than Eden* (Crossway, 2018); Timothy Brindle, *The Unfolding* (Lamp Mode Publishing, 2017); G. K. Beale, *A New Testament Biblical Theology: The Unfolding of the Old Testament in the New* (Baker Academic, 2011); Meredith G. Kline, *Kingdom Prologue: Genesis Foundations for a Covenantal Worldview* (Wipf and Stock, 2006); Meredith G. Kline, *God, Heaven and Har Magedon: A Covenantal Tale of Cosmos and Telos* (Wipf and Stock, 2006); Vos, *Biblical Theology*; Thomas R. Schreiner, *The King in His Beauty: A Biblical Theology of the Old and New Testaments* (Baker Academic, 2013); Herman Ridderbos, *Paul: An Outline of His Theology* (William B. Eerdmans, 1966).

[6] Vos, *Biblical Theology*, 5-9, 14-18. See also: Guy Prentiss Waters, *The Lord's Supper as the Sign and Meal of the New Covenant* (Crossway, 2019), 16.

[7] Brindle, *The Unfolding*, 7.

[8] See: Guthrie, *Even Better Than Eden*.

[9] Resources for Systematic Theology include: Herman Bavinck, *Reformed Dogmatics*, vols. 1-4, ed. by John Bolt, trans. by John Vriend (Baker Academic, 2003-2008); Francis Turretin, *Institutes of Elenctic Theology*, vols. 1-3, ed. by James T. Dennison, Jr., trans. by George Musgrave Giger (P&R, 1992-1997); Geerhardus Vos, *Reformed Dogmatics*, vols. 1-5, trans. and ed. by Richard B. Gaffin, Jr. (Lexham Press, 2012-2014); Robert Letham, *Systematic Theology* (Crossway, 2019); John Murray, *Collected Writings of John Murray*, vol. 2: Systematic Theology (Banner of Truth, 1977; reprint 2009); Louis Berkhof, *Systematic Theology* (GLH Publishing, reprint 2017); B. B. Warfield, *Bible Doctrines* (1929; Banner of Truth, 1988; reprint 2002).

[10] Michael Horton, *The Christian Faith: A Systematic Theology for Pilgrims on the Way* (Zondervan, 2011), 1001.

[11] Vos, *Biblical Theology*, 16. Richard Gaffin elaborates, "Biblical theology is concerned with the redemptive-historical plot as it actually unfolds scene by scene and over time. With an eye to that entire plot, systematic theology considers the roles of the primary actors, God and man. It highlights the constants that mark their characters as well as the dynamics of their ongoing activities and interactions." Richard B. Gaffin, Jr., "Systematic Theology and Hermeneutics," in *Seeing Christ in All of Scripture: Hermeneutics at Westminster Theological Seminary*, ed. by Peter Lillback (WSP, 2016), 50.

[12] Richard B. Gaffin, Jr., "Systematic Theology and Hermeneutics," 39.

[13] This is the language of the Chalcedonian Formula. See: Carl R. Trueman, *The Creedal Imperative* (Crossway, 2012), 100; cf. 99-102.

[14] Resources for Historical Theology include: Gregg R. Allison, *Historical Theology: An Introduction to Christian Doctrine* (Zondervan, 2011); Carl R. Trueman, *The Creedal Imperative* (Crossway, 2012); Joel R. Beeke and Mark Jones, *A Puritan Theology: Doctrine for Life* (Reformation Heritage Books, 2012); Heinrich Dezinger, *Compendium of Creeds, Definitions, and Declarations on Matters of Faith and Morals,* ed. by Peter Hünermann, 43rd ed. (Ignatius Press, 2010); Jaroslav Pelikan, *The Christian Tradition: A History of the Development of Doctrine*, vols. 1-5 (The University of Chicago Press, 1971-

1991); Daniel R. Hyde, *With Heart and Mouth: An Exposition of the Belgic Confession* (Reformed Fellowship, 2008); Richard A. Muller, *Post-Reformation Dogmatics*, vols. 1-4, 2nd ed. (Baker Academic, 2003); Robert Louis Wilken, *The Spirit of Early Christian Thought: Seeking the Face of God* (Yale, 2003); Alexander Roberts, James Donaldson, and Henry Wace, eds., *The Early Church Fathers*, vols. 1-38 (Hendrickson, 1994).

15 Allison, *Historical Theology,* 23. Emphasis added.

16 R. C. Sproul, *What is Reformed Theology? Understanding the Basics* (Baker, 1997), 52, 54-55.

17 Alister E. McGrath, "The Importance of Tradition for Modern Evangelicalism," in *Doing Theology for the People of God,* ed. by Donald Lewis and Alister E. McGrath (InterVarsity, 1996), 167.

18 Liturgical Forms and Prayers of the United Reformed Churches in Northern America Together with the Doctrinal Standards of the URCNA (The United Reformed Churches in North America [Canada], 2018), 139-141; Grudem, *Systematic Theology,* 1168-1171.

19 Trueman, *The Creedal Imperative,* 80.

20 See: Ibid., 12-80.

21 Resources in Practical Theology include: Jeramie Rinne, *Church Elders: How to Shepherd God's People* (Crossway, 2014); Richard Baxter, *The Reformed Pastor* (Banner of Truth, 1974; reprint 2012); Martin Bucer, *Concerning the True Care of Souls,* trans. by Peter Beale (Banner of Truth, 2009; reprint 2016); Edmund P. Clowney, *Preaching Christ in All of Scripture* (Crossway, 2003); Thomas J. Nettles, *Living By Revealed Truth: The Life and Pastoral Theology of Charles Haddon Spurgeon* (Mentor, 2013); Ichabod Spencer, *A Pastor's Sketches: Conversations with Anxious Souls Concerning the Way of Salvation* (Solid Ground Christian Books, 2013); W. Robert Godfrey, *Saving the Reformation: The Pastoral Theology of the Canons of Dort* (Reformation Trust, 2019); Jeremy Pierre and Deepak Reju, *The Pastor and Counseling: The Basics of Shepherding Members in Need* (Crossway, 2015); Stuart Scott and Heath Lambert, eds., *Counseling the Hard Cases: True Stories Illustrating the Sufficiency of God's Resources in Scripture* (B&H, 2012); David Powlison, *Seeing With New Eyes: Counseling and the Human Condition Though the Lens of Scripture* (P&R, 2003); Jonathan Gibson and Mark Earngey, *Reformation Worship: Liturgies from the Past for the Present* (New Growth Press, 2018); Charles Bridges, *The Christian Ministry: An Inquiry into the Cause if its Inefficiency* (The Banner of Truth, 2009); Joel Beeke, *Reformed Preaching: Proclaiming God's Word from the Heart of the Preacher to the Heart of His People* (Crossway, 2018); The Trinity Psalter Hymnal (Committee on Christian Education of the Orthodox Presbyterian Church and the Board of Directors of the United Reformed Churches in North America [USA], 2018); Jay Adams, *Competent to Counsel: Introduction to Nouthetic Counseling* (Zondervan, 1970); Nicholas Alford, *Doxology: How Worship Works* (Free Grace Press, 2017); Richard C. Barcellos, *The Lord's Supper as a Means of Grace: More Than a Memory* (Mentor, 2013); R. Kent Hughes, *The Pastor's Book: A Comprehensive and Practical Guide to Pastoral Ministry,* ed. by Douglas Sean O'Donnell (Crossway, 2015);

George Henry Gerberding, *The Lutheran Catechist* (The Lutheran Publication Society, 1910); Herold L. Senkbeil, *The Care of Souls: Cultivating a Pastor's Heart* (Lexham, 2019).

[22] See: Ligon Duncan, "The Ordinary Means of Growth," Ligonier (1 October 2007), https://www.ligonier.org/learn/articles/ordinary-means-growth/.

[23] I am indebted to Lane Tipton, who taught this concept in a Doctrine of Christ class at Westminster Theological Seminary in the spring of 2017. This is a slightly modified version of a diagram that Tipton presented in class.

[24] See also: Moises Silva, "The Case for Calvinistic Hermeneutics," in *Revelation and Reason: New Essays in Reformed Apologetics*, ed. by K. Scott Oliphint and Lane G. Tipton (P&R, 2007), 74-94.

[25] "Holy Bible, Book Divine," in the Trinity Hymnal: Baptist Edition (Great Commission Publications, 1995), 674.

Chapter 17

[1] "Discipline" can come in various forms, with both positive and negative aspects. In what follows, I focus more on the negative (corrective) side of discipline because it seems to be the most debated, misunderstood, and misused.

[2] Tripp goes on to say, "The issue is not a parental insistence on being obeyed. The issue is the child's need to be rescued from death—the death that results from rebellion left unchallenged in the heart.... The rod is a parent, in faith toward God and faithfulness toward his or her children, undertaking the responsibility of careful, timely, measured, and controlled use of physical punishment to underscore the importance of obeying God, thus rescuing the child from continuing in his foolishness until death.... The use of the rod is an act of faith. God has mandated its use. The parent obeys, not because he perfectly understands how it works, but because God has commanded it. The use of the rod is a profound expression of confidence in God's wisdom and the excellence of his counsel." Tedd Tripp, *Shepherding a Child's Heart* (Shepherd Press, 1995; revised, 2005), 103-105.

[3] Martha Peace and Stuart Scott, *The Faithful Parent: A Biblical Guide to Raising a Family* (P&R, 2010), 59.

[4] Sheol/Hades leads to Hell. See: Revelation 20:14; Geerhardus Vos, *Reformed Dogmatics*, vol. 5, trans and ed. by Richard B. Gaffin, Jr. (Lexham, 2016), 5:261-264; Derek W. H. Thomas, *Heaven on Earth: What the Bible Teaches about Life to Come* (Christian Focus, 2018), 24.

[5] Joel R. Beeke, *Parenting by God's Promises: How to Raise Children in the Covenant of Grace* (Reformation Trust, 2011), 154.

[6] Ibid., 146.

[7] Ibid., 155-156, 164.

[8] Richard Baxter, *The Reformed Pastor* (1656; The Banner of Truth, 2012), 58.

[9] George Henry Gerberding, *The Lutheran Catechist* (The Lutheran Publication Society, 1910), 170.

[10] Family Resources: J. Brandon Burks, *Internalizing the Faith: A Pilgrim's Catechism* (Fontes Press, 2018); Joel R. Beeke, ed., *Family Worship Bible Guide* (Reformation Heritage Books, 2016); Donald S. Whitney, *Family Worship: In the Bible, in History, and in Your Home* (Crossway, 2016); Carl Laferton, *The Garden, the Curtain, and the Cross* (The Good Book Company, 2016).

[11] "It is not a matter of asking whether the church or the family is to be the focal point of catechesis. Rather, it is essential that both take on that critical role, though each in their own way. God charged both the Church in an institutional sense and the family in an individual sense to step fully into the center of the catechesis of its members. Because cultural and religious identity were so critically important in ancient Israel, this task of teaching the faith within the family would likely have been viewed as the most important role for parents right after providing for shelter and food. God's instruction for parents to teach their children takes place in Deuteronomy 4 in the context of His establishment of a covenant with His people. This places their teaching of the faith as a core part of this covenantal connection between the people and their God." David L. Rueter, *Teaching the Faith at Home: What Does This Mean? How Is This Done?* (Concordia, 2016), 34.

[12] See: John Bunyan, *The Fear of God*, Puritan Paperbacks (The Banner of Truth, 2018).

[13] Bruce K. Waltke, *The Book of Proverbs: Chapters 1-15*, The New International Commentary on the Old Testament (William B. Eerdmans, 2004), 181.

[14] Polycarp, "The Epistle of Polycarp to the Philippians," in *Writings of the Apostolic Fathers: Mathetes, Polycarp, Barnabas, and Papias*, ed. by Alexander Roberts and James Donaldson (Veritatis Splendor Publications, 2014), 47.

[15] Joel Beeke, *Revelation*, The Lectio Continua Expository Commentary on the New Testament (Reformation Heritage Books, 2016), 391, 393.

[16] Nicolas Alford, *Doxology: How Worship Works* (Free Grace Press, 2017), 77.

[17] Calvin was not speaking in a Roman Catholic way but acknowledging that the church is the place where the children of God are nurtured, fed, and matured. John W. Tweeddale, "The Church as Mother," in *John Calvin: For a New Reformation*, ed. by Derek W. H. Thomas and John W. Tweeddale (Crossway, 2019), 476; cf. 471-488.

[18] Jonathan Leeman, *Church Membership: How the World Knows Who Represents Jesus* (Crossway, 2012), 75.

[19] Kent Hughes writes, "All churches have liturgies, even those which would call themselves 'non-liturgical.' In fact, having no liturgy is a liturgy! Relaxed charismatic services may be as liturgical in their format as a high-church service—and in some cases more rigid." Douglas Sean O'Donnell, "Sunday Worship," in *The Pastor's Book: A Comprehensive and Practical Guide to Pastoral Ministry* by R. Kent Hughes (Crossway, 2015), 42. This is what the Christian Reformed Church said of "liturgy" in their 1968 report on worship: "Liturgy is what people do when they worship.... Every church has

a liturgy, whether it worships with set forms inherited from the ages or whether it worships in the freedom of the moment. The only question is whether we have the best possible liturgy: it is never whether we have a liturgy." D. G. Hart and John R. Meuther, *With Reverence and Awe: Returning to the Basics of Reformed Worship* (P&R, 2002), 92-93.

[20] See: G. K. Beale, *We Become What We Worship: A Biblical Theology of Idolatry* (IVP, 2008). Of course, this is not in an "ontological" sense but in an "analogical" sense. We become *like* what we worship.

[21] Alford, *Doxology*, 3.

[22] The Regulative Principle of Worship means that we worship God according to the Bible. The Westminster Confession of Faith put it well: "The light of nature showeth that there is a God, who hath lordship and sovereignty over all, is good, and doth good unto all, and is therefore to be feared, loved, praised, called upon, trusted in, and served, with all the heart, and with all the soul, and with all the might. But the acceptable way of worshiping the true God is instituted by himself, and so limited by his own revealed will, that he may not be worshiped according to the imaginations and devices of men, or the suggestions of Satan, under any visible representation, or any other way not prescribed in the Holy Scripture." The Trinity Psalter Hymnal (Committee on Christian Education of the Orthodox Presbyterian Church and the Board of Directors of the United Reformed Churches in North America [USA], 2018), 932. The First and Second Commandments impact our worship of God. Begg said it well, "The first commandment forbids the worship of any false god, and the second demands that we do not worship the true God in an unworthy manner. It is not enough to worship the correct God. We must worship the correct God *correctly!*" Alistair Begg, *Pathway to Freedom: How God's Laws Guide Our Lives* (Moody, 2003), 64.

[23] Said by St. Prosper of Aquitaine. Quoted in: Jordan Cooper, *Liturgical Worship: A Lutheran Introduction* (Just and Sinner, 2018), 9.

[24] Ibid.

[25] For an explanation of the phrase "Spirit and truth," see: G. K. Beale, *A New Testament Biblical Theology: The Unfolding of the Old Testament in the New* (Baker, 2011), 134-135.

[26] While Thomas O'Loughlin writes in a more progressive Catholic arena, he is essentially right when he says: "Growth in faith and belonging is growth in a relationship with God.... Good liturgy can feed this life of faith, renew it and deepen it, and most people whose own faith-journeys have grown deeper affirm that this has been sustained and supported—among many other ways—by the liturgy." Thomas O'Loughlin, *The Rites and Wrongs of Liturgy: Why Good Liturgy Matters* (Liturgical Press, 2018), 10.

[27] Hart and Meuther, *With Reverence and Awe*, 95-102.

[28] Harold L. Senkbeil, *The Care of Souls: Cultivating a Pastor's Heart* (Lexham, 2019), 188.

[29] "If we can ever legitimately make ourselves the subject of a sentence containing the phrase 'do church,' it is only in a very subordinate and derivative way. The church that

takes God's grace seriously believes that the church is solely God's creature—not our response to his grace." Carl R. Trueman, *Grace Alone—Salvation as a Gift of God*, ed. by Matthew Barrett (Zondervan, 2017), 157-166; Trueman, *Luther on the Christian Life*, 158.

[30] The New Testament shows us that the early church prized the Psalms, even over other hymns and contemporary music. While the church can sing songs that have been written throughout the church age, so long as they are true and edifying, the Psalms ought to have a special place in our worship. After all, the Psalms are about Christ. Acts 16:25 records, "Now at midnight Paul and Silas prayed, and sung Psalms unto God: and the prisoners heard them" (GNV, 1599). In fact, the phrase "psalms and hymns and spiritual songs" in Colossians 3:16 likely refers solely to the Psalter. See: G. K. Beale, *Colossians and Philemon*, Baker Exegetical Commentary on the New Testament (Baker Academic, 2019), 305-306; cf. 302-307.

[31] This is just one example and not a set standard. See: Hart and Meuther, *With Reverence and Awe*, 98-100; Jonathan Gibson and Mark Earngey, *Reformation Worship: Liturgies from the Past for the Present* (New Growth Press, 2018).

[32] Mike Cosper, *Rhythms of Grace: How the Church's Worship Tells the Story of the Gospel* (Crossway, 2013), 125.

[33] See: Camden Bucey, Glen Clary, and Jim Cassidy, "The Order of Worship," Christ the Center, Reformed Forum (29 May 2015), https://reformedforum.org/ctc387/.

[34] "Come, Thou Fount of Every Blessing," by Robert Robinson, in The Trinity Psalter Hymnal, 429.

[35] "Immortal, Invisible, God Only Wise," by Walter C. Smith, in the Trinity Hymnal: Baptist Edition (Great Commission Publications, 1995), 35.

[36] "Rock of Ages, Cleft for Me," by Augustus Toplady, in the Trinity Psalter Hymnal, 452.

[37] As a Lutheran, Rueter has a different conception of the Sacraments, and our liturgies may also differ. However, the basic thrust of what he says here can be affirmed by the Reformed community. Rueter, *Teaching the Faith at Home*, 21.

[38] "In short, the end of Christ's intercession is the salvation of the elect. Through his death he purchased a right to his people and the benefits of their salvation. However, his intercession remains necessary to actually bring us into possession of all spiritual blessings, and ultimately heaven. In other words, the application of all Christ's work for his people depends, in the final analysis, upon his intercession. Without it, there is no salvation." Mark Jones, *Knowing Christ* (Banner of Truth, 2015), 178.

[39] Grace should not be understood as a substance or a thing. Vos explains: "Everything that happens in us or to us as the outworking of the attribute of God and the gift of grace in Christ is called grace in the specific sense of the word. And this third grace is in view when we speak of the *means of grace*. There are certain instruments by which God wills for us to come to know and to apply His favor residing in Christ. These are means connected with the communication of grace. Grace is hereby taken in its widest sense, so that it is not limited effectual, seeking, or regenerating

grace, but includes everything that happens subjectively in or below our conscious-ness.... the order and regularity that God follows in the working of grace is not a mystical one, set for it by a life process, but an objective, outward one, determined by the ministry of God's covenant according to Scripture.... grace makes use of the means, and is served by them, but is not identical with the means." Vos, *Reformed Dogmatics,* 5:77, 78, 80.

[40] Richard C. Barcellos, *The Lord's Supper as a Means of Grace: More Than a Memory* (Christian Focus, 2013), 55-71.

[41] Carl R. Trueman, *Grace Alone,* 160-161

[42] Ibid., 238.

[43] Barcellos, *The Lord's Supper as a Means of Grace,* 23-24.

[44] The Belgic Confession, Article 29, distinguishes a true church from a false church: "We believe that we ought to discern diligently and very carefully, by the Word of God, what is the true church—for all sects in the world today claim for themselves the name of 'the church.' We are not speaking here of the company of hypocrites who are mixed among the good in the church and who nonetheless are not part of it, even though they are physically there. But we are speaking of distinguishing the body and fellowship of the true church from all sects that call themselves 'the church.' The true church can be recognized if it has the following marks: The church engages in the pure preaching of the gospel; it makes use of the pure admin-istration of the sacraments as Christ instituted them; it practices church discipline for correcting faults. In short, it governs itself according to the pure Word of God, rejecting all things contrary to it and holding Jesus Christ as the only Head. By these marks one can be assured of recognizing the true church—and no one ought to be separated from it. As for those who can belong to the church, we can recognize them by the distinguishing marks of Christians: namely by faith, and by their fleeing from sin and pursuing righteousness, once they have received the one and only Savior, Jesus Christ. They love the true God and their neighbors, without turning to the right or left, and they crucify the flesh and its works. Though great weakness remains in them, they fight against it by the Spirit all the days of their lives, appeal-ing constantly to the blood, suffering, death, and obedience of the Lord Jesus, in whom they have forgiveness of their sins, through faith in him. As for the false church, it assigns more authority to itself and its ordinances than to the Word of God; it does not want to subject itself to the yoke of Christ; it does not administer the sacraments as Christ commanded in his Word; it rather adds to them or sub-tracts from them as it pleases; it bases itself on humans, more than on Jesus Christ; it persecutes those who live holy lives according to the Word of God and who re-buke it for its faults, greed, and idolatry. These two churches are easy to recognize and thus to distinguish from each other."

[45] WSC Q.88: "The outward and ordinary means whereby Christ communicateth to us the benefits of redemption are, his ordinances, especially the Word, sacraments, and

prayer; all which are made effectual to the elect for salvation." The Westminster Shorter Catechism in the Trinity Psalter Hymnal, 974.

[46] The Westminster Larger Catechism expresses this well in Q. 155: "How is the word made effectual to salvation? A. The Spirit of God maketh the reading, but especially the preaching of the word, an effectual means of enlightening, convincing, and humbling sinners; of driving them out of themselves, and drawing them unto Christ; of conforming them to his image, and subduing them to his will; of strengthening them against temptations and corruptions; of building them up in grace, and establishing their hearts in holiness and comfort through faith unto salvation." The Orthodox Presbyterian Church, accessed 14 January 2020, https://opc.org/lc.html.

[47] "Chapter One: Of the Holy Scripture Being the True Word of God," The Second Helvetic Confession, Christian Classics Ethereal Library, accessed 11 November 2019, https://www.ccel.org/creeds/helvetic.htm.

[48] Carl Trueman uses a similar analogy about his Latin classes he took as a young boy. Carl R. Trueman, "The Word as a Means of Grace," SBJT 19.4 (2015): 59-78, accessed 24 June 2019, https://faculty.wts.edu/wp-content/uploads/2016/05/The-Word-as-a-Means-of-Grace.pdf.

[49] Ibid.

[50] I prefer the word "sacrament" over the word "ordinance." J. I. Packer explains the word: "*Sacrament* is from the Latin word *sacramentum*, meaning a holy rite in general and in particular a soldier's sacred oath of allegiance. Study of the rites themselves yields the concept of a sacrament as a ritual action instituted by Christ in which signs perceived through the senses set forth to us the grace of God in Christ and the blessings of his covenant. They communicate, seal, and confirm possession of those blessings to believers, who by responsively receiving the sacraments give expression to their faith and allegiance to God.... The sacraments are rightly viewed as means of grace, for God makes them means to faith, using them to strengthen faith's confidence in his promises and to call forth acts of faith for receiving the good gifts signified. The efficacy of the sacraments to this end resides not in the faith or virtue of the minister but in the faithfulness of God, who, having given signs, is now pleased to use them. Knowing this, Christ and the apostles not only speak of the sign as if it were the thing signified but speak too as if receiving the former is the same as receiving the latter (e.g., Matt. 26:26-28; 1 Cor. 10:15-21; 1 Pet. 3:21-22). As the preaching of the Word makes the gospel audible, so the sacraments make it visible, and God stirs up faith by both means." J. I. Packer, *Concise Theology: A Guide to Historic Christian Beliefs* (Tyndale House, 1993), 209-210; Turretin also said it well: "As God willed to enter into a covenant with the church (of which we have thus far spoken) in order to apply to her the salvation purchased by Christ, so (such is his goodness) for the greater confirmation of faith, he has condescended to seal this covenant by sacraments as seals, that by them as badges he might distinguish and separate his people from the rest of the world." Francis Turretin, *Institutes of Elenctic Theology*, vol. 3, trans. by George Musgrave Giger, ed. by James T. Dennison Jr. (P&R, 1997), 3:337.

[51] Hercules Collins, *An Orthodox Catechism: Being the Sum of Christian Religion, Contained in the Law and Gospel*, ed. by Michael A. G. Haykin and G. Stephen Weaver, Jr. (Palmdale, CA: RBAP, 2014), 73-74. It was not uncommon for Particular Baptists to use the word "sacrament" (cf. William Kiffin and Benjamin Beddome), nor was it unusual for a Particular Baptist to define the sacraments as both *signs* and *seals* (cf. Christopher Blackwood). See: Samuel D. Renihan, *From Shadow to Substance: The Federal Theology of the English Particular Baptists (1642-1704)*, Centre for Baptist History and Heritage Studies, vol. 16, (Regents Park College, 2018), 92; Barcellos, *The Lord's Supper as a Means of Grace*, 114; Benjamin Beddome, *A Scriptural Exposition of the Baptist Catechism* (1776; Solid Ground Christian Books, 2006), 161-177.

[52] Herman Bavinck said sacraments are "visible, holy signs and seals instituted by God so that he might make believers understand more clearly and reassure them of the promises and benefits of the covenant of grace, and believers on their part might confess and confirm their faith and love before God, angels, and humankind." Herman Bavinck, *Reformed Dogmatics,* vol. 4, ed. by John Bolt, trans. by John Vriend (Baker Academic, 2008), 4:473; cf. 473-490. See also: Vos, *Reformed Dogmatics,* 5:157. Regarding the efficacy of the sacraments, the Reformed reject that the sacraments work *ex opere operato*. See: Francis Turretin, *Institutes of Elenctic Theology*, 3:363-369.

[53] See: Samuel Renihan, *The Mystery of Christ: His Covenant and His Kingdom* (Flounders, 2019), 203-206.

[54] "The Baptist Catechism," in *Teaching Truth, Training Hearts: The Study of Catechisms in Baptist Life*, revised ed., ed. by Thomas J. Nettles and Steve Weaver (Founders, 2017), 141.

[55] The Christian has already received justifying grace. The sacraments do not convert. Instead, they sanctify and strengthen. Bavinck said, "Baptismal grace exists and can, according to Scripture and the Reformed confession, exist in nothing other than in declaration and confirmation." Bavinck, *Reformed Dogmatics,* 4:521.

[56] Why does the Bible sometimes seem to link sacraments with the forgiveness or cleansing of sin? "The apostle says that God has saved us through baptism, since in sacramental phraseology the thing signified can be expressed by the sign." Vos, *Reformed Dogmatics,* 5:147. The Heidelberg Catechism Q.73 asks, "Why then does the Holy Spirit call baptism the water of rebirth and the washing away of sins? Answer: God has good reason for these words. To begin with, he wants to teach us that the blood and Spirit of Christ takes away our sins just as water removes dirt from the body. But more importantly, he wants to assure us, by this divine pledge and sign, that we are as truly washed of our sins spiritually as our bodies are washed with water physically." The Heidelberg Catechism in the Trinity Psalter Hymnal, 884.

[57] See: Thomas Vincent, *The Shorter Catechism Explained from Scripture*, Puritan Paperbacks (Banner of Truth, 2010), 242; Regarding the efficacy of the sacraments, the Reformed reject that the sacraments work *ex opere operato*. See: Turretin, *Institutes*, 3:363-369. Clowney writes, "A sacrament is a sign of *participation* in *saving* grace. It

marks not simply the presence and work of God, but his application of salvation to sinners." Edmund P. Clowney, *The Church*, Contours of Christian Theology (IVP, 1995), 271.

[58] John Calvin, *The Institutes of the Christian Religion*, vol. 2, trans. by Ford Lewis Battles, ed. by John T. McNeill (Westminster John Knox, 1960), IV.14.9.

[59] Bavinck, *Reformed Dogmatics*, 4:476-477.

[60] See: R. Scott Clark, "What Do We Mean by *Sacrament, Sign*, and *Seal*," Heidelblog, 8 July, 2018, https://heidelblog.net/2018/07/what-do-we-mean-by-sacrament-sign-and-seal/.

[61] Vos, *Reformed Dogmatics*, 5:98-99.

[62] Vincent, *The Shorter Catechism Explained from Scripture*, 244. Clowney writes, "A sacrament is a sign of *participation* in *saving* grace. It marks not simply the presence and work of God, but his application of salvation to sinners." Clowney, *The Church*, 271; Nevertheless, we ought not see the *efficacy* of the sacraments as being linked to the mere 'sacramental act.' Letham says, "The classic Reformed confessions regard the sacraments as means of grace, conveying blessings to faithful recipients. Their efficacy resides not in the sacramental elements or in the sacramental action, nor in the character or intention of the one who administers them, but in Christ's blessing and the working of the Spirit in the beneficiaries. They are means of grace only to those who fulfill the condition of the covenant of which they are signs and seals." Robert Letham, *Systematic Theology* (Crossway, 2019), 645.

[63] Vos, *Reformed Dogmatics*, 5:82, 90, 96, 99, 147, 151-154, 212, 220, 222, 230-233.

[64] "Nevertheless, the sacraments have great value. Because we are not [disembodied] spirits but sensuous earthly creatures who can only understand spiritual things when they come to us in humanly perceptible forms, God instituted the sacraments in order that by seeing those signs we might gain a better insight into his benefits, receive a stronger confirmation of his promises, and thus be supported and strengthened in our faith. The sacraments do not work faith but reinforce it, as a wedding ring reinforces love. They do not infuse physical grace but confer the whole Christ, whom believers already possess by the Word. They bestow on them the same Christ in another way and by another road and so strengthen the faith. Furthermore, they renew the believers' covenant with God, strengthen them in the communion with Christ, join them more closely to each other, set them apart from the world, and witness to the angels and their fellow human beings, [showing] that they are the people of God, the church of Christ, the communion of saints." Bavinck, *Reformed Dogmatics*, 4:489-490.

[65] Vos, *Reformed Dogmatics*, 5:231.

[66] Bavinck, *Reformed Dogmatics*, 4:578.

[67] Vos, *Reformed Dogmatics*, 5:231

[68] Barcellos, *The Lord's Supper as a Means of Grace*, 85.

[69] Vos, *Reformed Dogmatics*, 5:154-156; Carl R. Trueman, *Luther on the Christian Life: Cross and Freedom* (Crossway, 2015), 142-144.

[70] Letham writes, "It may be tempting to think of the sacraments as merely human rites. However, the sacraments are preeminently signs for God, indicating what he has done or will do. They go beyond the surface appearance and bring us into direct contact with eternal realities in which the grace of God is powerful at work.... Baptism is into the one name of the Father, the Son, and the Holy Spirit; it belongs to God. The indivisible action of all three persons of the Trinity is the theme." Letham, *Systematic Theology*, 637-638. See also: Robert Kolb and Carl R. Trueman, *Between Wittenberg and Geneva: Lutheran and Reformed Theology in Conversation* (Baker Academic, 2017), 166-167. Reformed Baptists likewise understand baptism to be a means of grace; however, they also believe that baptism is always a profession of one's faith, since infants are never baptized. Renihan writes, "On the one hand, it is God's visible promise that all who are in His Son are new creations by virtue of their union with Christ in His death and resurrection (Romans 6:3-5). And on the other hand, it is the individual's profession of faith in those very promises (1 Peter 3:21-22)." Samuel Renihan, *The Mystery of Christ*, 204.

[71] The Heidelberg Catechism Q.69, United Reformed Churches in North America, accessed 14 January 2020, https://threeforms.org/heidelberg-catechism/.

[72] Bavinck, *Reformed Dogmatics*, 4:579.

[73] "Now in the Lord's Supper bread and wine represent the very body and blood of Christ. The reason hereof is this. As bread nourisheth and strengtheneth man, and giveth him ability to labour; so the body of Christ, eaten by faith, feedeth and satisfieth the soul of man, and furnisheth the whole man to all duties of godliness. As wine is drink to the thirsty, and maketh merry the hearts of men; so the blood of our Lord Jesus, drunken by faith, doth quench the thirst of the burning conscience, and filleth the hearts of the faithful with unspeakable joy. But in the action of the supper the bread of the Lord is broken, the wine is poured out. For the body of our Saviour was broken, that is, by all means afflicted, and his blood gushed and flowed plentifully out of his gaping wounds. And we ourselves truly do break with our own hands the bread of the Lord; for we ourselves are in fault that he was torn and tormented. Our sins wounded him, and we ourselves crucified him; that is to say, he was crucified for us, that by his death he might deliver us from death.... By this short treatise touching the analogy I think it is plain, that sacraments stir up and help the faith of the godly.... sacraments are now also outwardly given, which do visibly represent those things to our eyes, and as it were make them to enter into our senses, which the mind inwardly comprehendeth, considereth, and meditateth upon. For because the whole action, which consisteth of the words and the rite or ceremony, is counted with the sign; our eyes see the signs and all things which are done in the whole action of the signs; all which do as it were speak: our ears hear the words and institutions of Christ: yea, our very touching and tasting, they also do feel and perceive how sweet and good the Lord is: so that now the whole man, as it were both body and soul, caught up into heaven, doth feel and perceive that his faith is stirred up and holpen, and, to be short, that the

fruit of faith in Christ is passing sweet and comfortable. All these things have place in them that believe." Henry Bullinger, *The Decades of Henry Bullinger, Minister of the Church of Zurich*, 5th Decade, trans. by H. I., ed. by Rev. Thomas Harding (1551; Cambridge, 1852), 329-331.

[74] Guy Prentiss Waters, *The Lord's Supper as the Sign and Meal of the New Covenant* (Crossway, 2019), 104, 113. Barcellos, *The Lord's Supper as a Means of Grace*, 68-69.

[75] Tertullian comments on prayer: "By delegated grace it turns away no feeling of pain, but it arms with endurance those who are suffering and knowing pain and grieving. It increases grace with bravery so that faith might know what it obtains from the Lord, understanding what it is suffering for the sake of the name of the Lord.... Prayer is the buttress of faith, our armor and weaponry against the enemy that watches us from every side. So never let us set out unarmed—let us remember the station by day and the vigil by night." Tertullian, "On Prayer," in *Tertullian, Cyprian, and Origen On the Lord's Prayer*, Popular Patristics Series (St. Vladimir's, 2004), 63-64.

[76] "Prayer is a means of grace because the economy of grace involves the intercession of Christ. That intercession, even now, is what makes God's grace a potent reality to individual Christians." Carl R. Trueman, *Grace Alone*, 221; cf. 220-223.

[77] Ibid., 225-227.

[78] WSC Q.98: "Prayer is an offering up of our desires unto God, for things agreeable to His will, in the name of Christ, with confession of our sins, and thankful acknowledgement of his mercies." The Westminster Shorter Catechism, the Trinity Psalter Hymnal, 975.

[79] Hart and Meuther, *With Reverence and Awe*, 142.

[80] As quoted in: Charles Spurgeon, "Prayer – The Forerunner of Mercy," The Spurgeon Center, accessed 24 June, 2019, https://www.spurgeon.org/resource-library/sermons/prayer-the-forerunner-of-mercy#flipbook/.

[81] You will notice the article: "*the* prayers." Cooper said, "Luke is not just referencing the practice of prayers in general, but the *prayers*. These are specific prayers which are being prayed, and most likely, either traditional Jewish prayers or a modified Christian form of those prayers. The point here is that the early Christians, when gathered together, had specific prayers which would be prayed at each meeting." Cooper, *Liturgical Worship*, 32. See also: O'Donnell, "Sunday Worship," 48.

[82] As quoted in: Michael Horton, *Ordinary: Sustainable Faith in a Radical, Restless World* (Zondervan, 2014), 20.

[83] Michael Horton, "The Means of Grace and Sanctification: Part I," Office Hours, Westminster Seminary California (24 February 2014), https://www.wscal.edu/resource-center/the-means-of-grace-and-sanctification-part-i

[84] Horton, *Ordinary*, 23.

[85] See: Camden Bucey, Jeff Waddington, and Jim Cassidy, "The Ordinary Means of Grace and the Local Church," Christ the Center, Reformed Forum (9 November 2018), https://reformedforum.org/ctc567/.

[86] There are implications for a church's life and ministry when a means-of-grace approach is adopted. This approach clashes with the more emotional, moral, and seeker approaches. I have disagreements with aspects of the Lutheran liturgy and I believe Cooper largely paints a straw-man regarding Reformed worship, but his explanation and critique of the emotionally-driven, morally-driven, and seeker-driven models is spot on. Though a means-of-grace approach is not against emotions, ethics, or welcoming unbelievers, it is distinct from these models. See: Cooper, *Liturgical Worship*, 10-14; Ligon Duncan, "The Ordinary Means of Growth," Ligonier Ministries (1 October 2007), https://www.ligonier.org/learn/articles/ordinary-means-growth/; Coleen Sharp, "Ordinary Means of Grace," Theology Gals (13 January 2019), http://theologygals.com/2019/01/ordinary-means-of-grace/; Bucey, Waddington, and Cassidy, "The Ordinary Means of Grace and the Local Church"; Michael Horton, "The Means of Grace and Sanctification: Part I"; Horton, "The Means of Grace and Sanctification: Part II," Office Hours, Westminster Seminary California (3 March 2014), https://www.wscal.edu/resource-center/the-means-of-grace-and-sanctification-part-ii.

[87] For a discussion of the "keys of the kingdom," see: J. Brandon Burks, *Internalizing the Faith: A Pilgrim's Catechism* (Fontes Press, 2018), 50.

[88] This doesn't mean that church members never vote on important matters but that, when they do vote, they are only permitted to vote the will of the King. In other words, their vote must be scripturally informed and not based on personal preference, public opinion, or the traditions of men.

[89] Jeramie Rinne, *Church Elders: How to Shepherd God's People Like Jesus* (Crossway, 2014), 16. Presbyterian and Reformed churches, however, will see a distinction between *teaching* elders and *ruling* elders. See: Clowney, *The Church*, 207-214.

[90] "Plurality acknowledges human limitations by recognizing that no one elder can possess the full complement of gifts God intends to use, bless, and build the church (1 Corinthians 12:21) .... the authority for the local church was given to the entire eldership, not just to one gifted leader. In other words, the responsibility inheres in the group, not the man." Dave Harvey, *Healthy Plurality = Durable Church: How-To Build and Maintain a Healthy Plurality of Elders* (Sojourn Network Press, 2018), 7-8. See also: Rinne, *Church Elders*, 86; Martin Bucer, *Concerning the True Care of Souls*, trans. by Peter Beale (Banner of Truth, 2009; reprint 2016), 35.

[91] Trueman, *Luther on the Christian Life*, 189, n.35.

[92] Gerberding, *The Lutheran Catechist*, 134.

[93] Harold L. Senkbeil, *The Cure of Souls: Cultivating a Pastor's Heart* (Lexham, 2019), 14. This should not, however, lead to an elitist understanding of pastoral ministry. See: Ibid., 24.

[94] Alford, *Doxology*, 102.

[94] "Christ Jesus Lay in Death's Strong Bands," by Martin Luther, trans. by Richard Massie, https://hymnary.org/text/christ_jesus_lay_in_deaths_strong_bands.

Chapter 18

[1] R. Scott Clark, "The Killer Bs: Idols of the Minister's Heart," Heidelblog, accessed 20 June 2019, https://heidelblog.net/2013/01/the-killer-bs-idols-of-the-ministers-heart-2/.

[2] Geerhardus Vos, "Heavenly-Mindedness," in *Grace and Glory: Sermons Preached in the Chapel of Princeton Theological Seminary* (Solid Ground Christian Books, 1922; reprint 2007), 150.

[3] Jonathan Edwards, "The Pilgrim's Life," in *The Works of Jonathan Edwards*, vol. 2 (Hendrickson, 2011), 243-246. Emphasis original.

[4] Our path is the narrow, righteous path. See: Ps 17:5; 25:4; 84:5; 94:18; 107:7; 119:101; Prov 2:13, 16-22; 4:25-27; 12:28; 15:10, 19, 21, 24; 16:25; 19:16; 21:16; 22:6; 23:19; Isa 35:8; Jer 18:15; Matt 7:13-14.

[5] John Bunyan, *The Pilgrim's Progress* (Answers in Genesis, 2006), 94-95.

[6] James Douglas Baird, "Introduction," in *In Defense of the Eschaton: Essays in Reformed Apologetics*, by William D. Dennison (Wipf and Stock, 2015), xxiii.

[7] "Who Would True Valor See," by John Bunyan, mod. by Pearcy Dearmer, http://www.hymntime.com/tch/htm/h/e/w/h/hewhowvb.htm.

CPSIA information can be obtained
at www.ICGtesting.com
Printed in the USA
LVHW051235090221
678815LV00015B/432